Praise fo
MARY MAGDALEN

"This book is a masterpiece. I haven't been this excited or awakened by a book for a decade. This is what it looks like when an artist follows her heart and her passion instead of the crowd."

— **Glennon Doyle**, #1 *New York Times* best-selling author of *Love Warrior*

"The evidence within these pages, both scholarly and lived experience, will change you on a cellular level as you remember what has been forgotten for thousands of years, but has never been untrue: that the feminine is sacred and holy. This book is a revolution."

— **Kate Northrup**, best-selling author of *Do Less* and *Money: A Love Story*

"Meggan Watterson is a modern-day prophetess who sets souls on fire with her lyrical prose and courageous truth-telling. Her unearthing of the hidden and silenced realities of the first apostle's life and legacy ignites revelations that will transform the hearts and minds of readers who are ready to claim their own power and spiritual authority."

— **Jamia Wilson**, author of *Step Into Your Power*
and executive director of The Feminist Press

"*Mary Magdalene Revealed* brings together the exquisite balance of personal experience and the uncovering of spiritual texts that quite simply rock and lovingly challenge the Christianity of the world today. Meggan Watterson is the spiritual teacher to spiritual teachers and this book is a road map to the heart of Christ's message."

— **Kyle Gray**, best-selling author of *Angel Prayers* and *Raise Your Vibration*

"Meggan Watterson is a conduit carrying the electrical charge of spirit and weaving this channeled energy into her work. She is a soul doula, gently holding our hands as we cross the river to spiritual healing and emotional salvation through these pages. If you ever wondered if the feminine is dormant in our spiritual traditions, *Mary Magdalene Revealed* makes it clear that our past, present, and future lies within her."

— **Latham Thomas**, founder of Mama Glow and author of *Own Your Glow*

"Fierce, raw, compelling, disruptive, and deep—Meggan Watterson has penned a classic. Read it . . . savor it . . . read it again, then let it change you."

— **Colette Baron-Reid**, best-selling author of *Uncharted*

"She is brave, she is beautiful, she is divine. Driven by passion, by a calling higher than she can see or know. She can deliver us all into a new stratosphere of love and divinity. Am I describing Mary Magdalene? Or Meggan Watterson? Both. They are sisters in this holy mission of bringing Mary's breathtakingly beautiful gospel to the world, today."

— **Regena Thomashauer**, *New York Times* best-selling author of *Pussy: A Reclamation*

"Like a feminist Indiana Jones, Meggan Watterson goes on a mystical adventure to uncover the hidden teachings of one of Christ's closest companions and disciples, Mary Magdalene, and her discovery could change history. "

— **Cheryl Richardson**, *New York Times* best-selling author of *The Art of Extreme Self Care*

"With deep honesty, soulful artistry, and intellectual rigor, Meggan brings us a picture of the real Mary Magdalene—the one who is alive in each of our hearts—and leads us through how to experience and live from the Christ in each of us in our daily lives."

— **Robert and Hollie Holden**, authors and teachers of *A Course in Miracles*

"After so much work, devotion, and innovation, Meggan Watterson deserves to be heard."

— **Hal Taussig, Ph.D.**, author and editor of *A New New Testament*

"*Mary Magdalene Revealed* is one of the most beautiful, powerful, exciting, and sorely needed books of our time. Fiercely honest and courageous, Watterson rejects the lies and limitations of patriarchal bias and resurrects the heartbeat of genuine love and intimacy with God and one another through the teachings and life of Mary Magdalene. I couldn't put it down!"

— **Sonia Choquette**, best-selling author of *Waking Up in Paris*

"I have been waiting to read *Mary Magdalene Revealed* my entire life. Its pages will reveal the humble power of your soul and a truth that can be felt but cannot be put into words."

— **Rebecca Campbell**, best-selling author of *Rise, Sister, Rise*

"It is rare to find a book that catalyzes a mystical awakening, a book that feels like a reunion with a long-lost key to your soul's evolution."

— **Sarah Drew**, best-selling author of *Gaia Codex*

"Meggan has given us an extraordinary gift. Through her compelling and courageous work, we are called back to ourselves as bodies, as spiritual beings, to our wholeness and fullness, helping us to find our inner voice which will ultimately set us free."

— **Celene Lillie, Ph.D.**, director of translation for *A New New Testament*

Mary Magdalene Revealed

Also by MEGGAN WATTERSON

*The Divine Feminine Oracle**

How to Love Yourself (and Sometimes Other People),
with Lodro Rinzler*

*REVEAL**

The Sutras of Unspeakable Joy

*Available from Hay House

Please visit:

Hay House USA: www.hayhouse.com®
Hay House Australia: www.hayhouse.com.au
Hay House UK: www.hayhouse.co.uk
Hay House India: www.hayhouse.co.in

MARY MAGDALENE REVEALED

The First Apostle, Her Feminist Gospel & the Christianity We Haven't Tried Yet

MEGGAN WATTERSON

HAY HOUSE LLC
Carlsbad, California • New York City
London • Sydney • New Delhi

Published in the United States by: Hay House LLC: www.hayhouse.com®
Published in Australia by: Hay House Australia Pty. Ltd.: www.hayhouse.com.au
Published in the United Kingdom by: Hay House UK, Ltd.: www.hayhouse.co.uk
Published in India by: Hay House Publishers India: www.hayhouse.co.in

Cover design: Mary Ann Smith • *Interior design:* Bryn Starr Best

Library of Congress has cataloged the earlier edition as follows:

Names: Watterson, Meggan, 1974- author.
Title: Mary Magdalene revealed : the first apostle, her feminist gospel & the Christianity we haven't tried yet / Meggan Watterson.
Description: 1st edition. | Carlsbad : Hay House, Inc., 2019. | Includes bibliographical references.
Identifiers: LCCN 2019014131 | ISBN 9781401954901 (hardcover : alk. paper)
Subjects: LCSH: Gospel of Mary--Criticism, interpretation, etc. | Mary Magdalene, Saint.
Classification: LCC BT1392.G652 W38 2019 | DDC 229/.8--dc23 LC record available at https://lccn.loc.gov/2019014131

Tradepaper ISBN: 978-1-4019-5428-4
E-book ISBN: 978-1-4019-5429-1
Audiobook ISBN: 978-1-4019-5430-7

19 18 17 16 15 14 13
1st edition, July 2019
2nd edition, January 2021

Printed in the United States of America

This product uses responsibly sourced papers and/or recycled materials. For more information, see www.hayhouse.com.

This book is for my son, Shai
—which means "gift" in Aramaic
In French, love at first sight is *coup de foudre*—
"lightning strikes"
This is what it felt like when I first saw you, Shai—
I recognized you
It felt like witnessing the proof of
a love that has always existed
My heart flipped inside out
and has been expanding ever since

Sister, we know that the Savior loved you more than all other women. Tell us the words of the Savior that you remember, the things which you know that we don't because we haven't heard them.

Mary responded, "I will teach you about what is hidden from you."

— THE GOSPEL OF MARY MAGDALENE

CONTENTS

INTRODUCTION

The Eye of the Heart

(Pages 1–6 are missing.)

— Mary 1:1

Mary Magdalene's gospel starts with missing pages. These are the words we can't get back, this is the wisdom, the voice of Christ from the heart of a woman, that was torn out and most likely destroyed before the rest of her gospel was buried. There was something so incendiary in these first six pages that her gospel starts on page seven.

And there's something poetic about that, since according to Mary's gospel, seven is the number of stages we need to go through, or powers we need to confront within ourselves, to reach a clarity or singularity of heart that lets us see past the ego of our own little lives to what's more real, and lasting, and infinite, and already here, within us.

Three copies of the Gospel of Mary have been recovered—two in Greek and one in Coptic. All three versions of her gospel are missing the beginning, and then also, four pages in the middle. And those four pages would have contained the answer to what

I believe is one of the most significant questions we could ever know. Mary asks Christ,

"So, now, Lord, does a person who sees a vision see it with the soul or with the spirit?"

All we have of his answer is this provocative yet cryptic start:

"The Savior answered, 'A person does not see with the soul or with the spirit. Rather the mind, which exists between the two, sees the vision and that is what . . .'"

"Mind," here, isn't the modern, dualistic concept of the mind that we think of today. It's not mind devoid of body. It's a word that's hard to translate from the Greek. It's actually best to keep it in Greek, although the first time I came across it, I thought it was in French. It's *nous*. *Nous* in French means we. *Nous* in Greek means the eye of the heart. It's the vision, or perception of the soul.

How we see anything, changes everything. And there's so much at stake here, which is why her question to Christ is still ours to answer. And which is why perhaps the answer to her brilliant question was torn from her gospel in the first place. Because it would have revealed to us how we perceive the divine directly, from within.

What's at stake is spiritual authority. And what I mean by that is both the struggle to determine who has the power to tell Mary Magdalene's story and, subsequently, the authority to tell the truth about our own story.

If how we see, truly see, is not with eyesight, but with a vision, a form of spiritual perception that allows us to know what's real, what's lasting, what's actually true, if this comes from within us; then no one has power over us.

Simple, right?

Yes. And, simply revolutionary.

For me, these seven powers in Mary's gospel serve as the template of what it means to be human. It's like being handed a road map for the inner terrain. Here are the seven routes the ego can (and most likely will) take while you're embodied. Here are the places as human beings we get stuck. These are the climates, the states of mind that can compel us to act in ways that are not indicative of who we really are. These are the powers that can silence us from within.

I guess this story I'm about to tell you is what religious scholars would call a "conversion story." The Gospel of Mary did convert me, or her gospel helped me understand why I've never felt at home in a Christianity that excluded it.

From a theological perspective, Mary Magdalene's gospel is considered an "ascent narrative," which means that it describes a path that we can navigate to liberate the soul; not in death, but here in this lifetime. The word *ascent*, though, is misleading in that the imagination immediately goes upward. Thinks transcendence. Ascension according to the Gospel of Mary is more accurately a descent into the heart; so farther up is actually further in.

For me, finding Mary Magdalene's voice meant recovering my own. This is why I've spent the majority of my life studying her gospel, and following her legend through history. I hope in sharing her voice in this book, you will hear the voice of your own soul. (Which might feel lofty, and intimidating, I know, but it's just this clear, calm, unassuming voice of love inside you.)

I also want to clarify that this is going to end the way it began. It's very T. S. Eliot and the Four Quartets: "And the end of all our exploring / Will be to arrive where we started / And know the place for the first time." It's not about getting somewhere, or reaching someplace else. Although I will tell you how I ended up perched like a baby goat in yoga gear on the side of a mountain in the South of France searching for Mary Magdalene's "Cave of Eggs."

The point of Mary's gospel is not to suggest that we need to become someone else, someone "better." There isn't this om-vibrating version of yourself that you figure out how to be by the end of this book, or that I've become by living it.

It's about acquiring a vision that allows us to see what has always been here, within us. It's about the quality and intensity of our existence. It's about the possibility of actually being present, instead of being caught without even realizing it in the endless stories the ego tells; from the second we wake up, dividing us from what's already right here, dividing us from each other and ourselves, dividing us from what we consider good, or god. It's about *really* waking up to the fact that our system of understanding the world is no longer serving us.

Or so this is how my conversion story goes. I wake up to a way I've been operating in the world, the world created by my ego; and I see the suffering it perpetuates. I see that there's another way.

And that way does not include finding some hot, saucy pants lover, who completes me (not so far anyway), or the discovery of a tried and true recipe for uninterrupted joy. Not fame. Not success. There's no end point here, no fixed state of completion. There's no master or guru status. It's just alpha, then omega, ad infinitum. This is what I'm trying to explain. There is no X marks the spot.

It's simpler than that, and far more difficult.

It's more of a series of perpetual moments when you remember that you don't have to feel separate from love—if you don't want to. Even in the midst of the worst of what we say to ourselves, even when someone we love most in the world can't see us at all, we can practice a way that humbles us, that disrupts the ego's grasp, and lets us return again, with ease (even eventually, with levity), to love.

It's all very quiet and unremarkable, though. It's not showy, or exciting. It's more like this, from Elizabeth Gilbert: "Never forget that once upon a time, in an unguarded moment, you recognized yourself as your friend."

And in that moment of recognition, this is when we save ourselves, from the self that was never real to begin with. This is when we see with the eye of the heart.

Why I Could Kiss a Copt

I am the first and the last. I am she who is honored and she who is scorned.
I am the whore and the holy woman. I am the wife and the virgin.
I am the bride and the bridegroom. I am she, the Lord.

— The Thunder, Perfect Mind 1:5–10

The earliest evidence of the lost gospel of Mary Magdalene was discovered in January 1896, at an antiquities market in Cairo, by a German scholar named Carl Reinhardt. It was written in Coptic on ancient papyrus. Coptic is an Egyptian language that is still used today by Egyptian Christians, called "Copts." It was placed in the Egyptian museum in Berlin with the official title and catalogue number of Codex Berolinensis 8502, which is a mouthful. So, scholars refer to it as the Berlin Codex.

Egyptologist Carl Schmidt set about creating a German translation of the gospel. Except for the missing pages, the text was in good condition. And since Coptic script was used almost exclusively by Copts, Schmidt concluded that their communities in Egypt were the ones to translate, preserve, and perhaps even to save the Gospel of Mary from complete erasure.

The publication of Schmidt's translation of the Gospel of Mary was ready to go to a printing press in Leipzig in 1912. But just as the printer was nearing completion, a water pipe burst and destroyed the entire first edition. Schmidt tried to salvage the mess but was interrupted by World War I. And then before he could return to Leipzig to resurrect the project, he died in 1938. He bequeathed the project to another scholar by the name of Walter Till.

In the meantime, in 1917, a small 3rd-century Greek fragment of the Gospel of Mary was found. It's known as Papyrus Rylands 463 and was also discovered in Egypt, at Oxyrhynchus.

This version added clearer confirmation to passages of the Berlin Codex and also additional evidence about the gospel's early date. Walter Till incorporated the new information into his translation of the Gospel of Mary. It was ready to go to print in 1943, but by this time, World War II made the publication of Mary's gospel, again, impossible. And then, Till gave up his attempts altogether.

When the war was over, there had been a discovery in a village called Nag Hammadi in Egypt of a large amount of early Christian scripture. For example, the Gospel of Thomas, the Gospel of Philip, and this powerful, and poetic piece of scripture called *The Thunder, Perfect Mind,* among many others.

No copies of the Gospel of Mary were found among the preserved texts at Nag Hammadi. However, the two texts that were found within the Berlin Codex rolled up with the Gospel of Mary appeared among the mass findings of manuscripts: *The Apocryphon of John* and *The Sophia of Jesus Christ.* These texts discovered at Nag Hammadi were collectively referred to as the "Gnostic Gospels," because they focus on *gnosis,* which is a Greek term meaning self-knowledge, or more specifically, the knowledge that comes from direct experience.

The label "Gnostic," though, created a misperception around these early Christian texts, and Mary's gospel got thrown into the confusion.

So, let's be clear: there is no such thing as "Gnosticism." There wasn't a cult of organized Gnostics these ancient texts define. These texts, including the Gospel of Mary, are evidence of the various forms of Christianities that existed before the 4th century when the current form of the bible was codified. I know I just made Christianity plural there. But this is what these ancient texts prove; there were many threads of Christianity in the wake of Christ. And one of those threads, let's call it a red one, believed women were as worthy as men to teach, and lead the church. But this wasn't (obviously) the thread that won out.

Here's a curious sympathy, or synchronicity; supposedly, these texts found at Nag Hammadi were smuggled from out of Egypt and sequestered for a while in the manuscript collection of the Swiss psychiatrist Carl Jung. This is fascinating, to me at least, because Jung believed that the church would die without the "Mother," and that the feminine had been "submerged" in our collective unconscious. He also wrote *The Red Book*, which is essentially his efforts to connect directly to his soul.

The commonality between all of these early Christian sacred texts found buried in Egypt is that they spoke of this hidden, more human, and feminine side of Christ, of Mary Magdalene's importance, and of salvation as an inward act of personal transformation.

The Nag Hammadi findings were at last released to a panel of international scholars to begin to assess their import and contribution to understanding the beliefs of some of the earliest Christians.[1] So, although Mary's gospel was found in 1896, the first print edition of her gospel wasn't published until 1955. Mary's gospel is the only gospel written in the name of a woman.

A third, and potentially final, version of the Gospel of Mary has been found, also in Greek, and also at Oxyrhynchus, in northern Egypt. This is a very significant discovery. As author, scholar, and Harvard Divinity professor Dr. Karen King explains in her translation of Mary's gospel, "Because it is unusual for several copies from such early dates to have survived, the attestation of the Gospel of Mary as an early Christian work is unusually strong."[2]

Episcopal priest, and author, Cynthia Bourgeault claims that if Dr. Karen King is correct, "this would place the Gospel of Mary Magdalene within the earliest strata of Christian writings, roughly contemporary with the Gospel of John."[3]

This arduous and somewhat calamitous process of Mary's gospel finally making its way into print feels significant to me. It reflects the almost magnetic reluctance of shifting our perspective about her, like the effort of what it would take for a river to change direction. And for me, it reflects the process of what it has taken me personally to share my truth about who she is and the truth about how her gospel has impacted my life.

As we make our way through each passage Mary's gospel contains, I've also included passages at the start of certain chapters from these three texts, the Gospel of Thomas, the Gospel of

Philip, and *The Thunder, Perfect Mind,* because they help to contextualize Mary's gospel. Her gospel wasn't this one-off, unicorn among horses, type of scripture. Reading it alongside these other gospels and early Christian scripture allows us to see that it was a part of a community of belief.

I've been trained as a theologian, which just means "a person who engages in the study of god." Or in my case, a person who engages in the study of all that has been left out of our ideas of god. I will draw from my direct experience, and illuminate each passage as far as I'm able to, and also move us through the legend of Mary Magdalene herself, and her misunderstood status as the penitent prostitute to reveal a much more historically and theologically accurate vision of who she was, and remains.

The seven powers mentioned in Mary's gospel (darkness, craving, ignorance, craving for death, enslavement to the physical body, the false peace of the flesh, and the compulsion of rage) are the precursors to Christianity's seven deadly sins (pride, greed, envy, gluttony, lust, sloth, and anger). And I believe, they are the "seven demons" that Luke 8:2 claims were expelled from Mary: "With him went the Twelve, as well as some women who had been healed of wicked spirits and of infirmities. They were Mary, known as Mary of Magdala (from whom seven demons had been expelled)."[4]

The emphasis of that passage is traditionally on the fact that Mary had to be healed of those seven "demons," but I like to focus on the fact that Mary was the first to be listed among the women who had been healed and that walked with Christ. These are the same seven powers, or "demons," that Pope Gregory in the 6th century proclaimed during his Homily 33 proved her "sinfulness." For me, rather than proving how far she "fell," I see the seven "demons" as proof of how much she overcame.

It feels important, potent maybe, to make a small yet conscious effort toward reparation. To repair our idea of Mary Magdalene, I'm going to move through the seven powers she teaches about in her gospel, and give my version of a homily, or a sermon. And by sermon, I don't mean a formal or official one; they're more like love letters.

And even though these seven powers will progress from the first to the seventh in a linear way in this book, they are meant to be understood as powers that circle back into our lives again and again, for some of us, several times a day. And each sermon-like-love-letter in a way will be a chance for me to practice a Christianity that never excluded Mary's gospel, and that understood these seven powers not as demonic or sinful but simply as human.

For the passages of Mary's gospel, I have referred to Dr. Karen L. King's translation from her seminal book, *The Gospel of Mary of Magdala: Jesus and the First Woman Apostle.* For the list of the seven powers translated from the Greek in Mary's gospel, I've preferred Cynthia Bourgeault's translation from her book *The Meaning of Mary Magdalene.* For the Gospel of Thomas, I have used Elaine Pagels's translation from *Beyond Belief: The Secret Gospel of Thomas.* And I have used Orthodox theologian Jean-Yves Leloup's translation of the Gospel of Philip, from his book *Jesus, Mary Magdalene and the Gnosis of Sacred Union.* Any passages from the New Testament that I quote or refer to are from Dr. Hal Taussig's *A New, New Testament: A Bible for the 21st Century Combining Traditional and Newly Discovered Texts.*

I came across the quote that opens this chapter from *The Thunder, Perfect Mind* in my early 20s before I found Mary's gospel, but in many ways, it led me to it. I read, "I am the whore and the holy woman," and my whole body applauded. I had to brace myself against the bookshelf from the shock and extreme relief I felt in the corner of the bookstore where I couldn't stop inhaling it. I had no idea what god was or wasn't, I had no clue that I would soon be devoting my life to feminist theology, but everything in me knew that this is what I had been missing.

This voice was raw, and contradictory, and powerful, and paradoxical, and made so much sense to me I wanted to scream sincerely for the first time in my life, "Hallelujah!"

I didn't understand why but finding this voice made these crazy rivulets of joy, these electric currents of energy, race through me.

My eyes read, and re-read, "I am she, the Lord."

We Can't Half-Ass Death

Every nature, every modeled form, every creature,
exists in and with each other.

— Mary 2:2

I was up in the middle of the night, several years ago, scrolling through the Internet like it had secrets to reveal to me. I clicked through to an article about a seed bank that's buried deep in a mountain in Norway. Supposedly, there are over 800,000 varieties of seeds from plants, to trees, to fruits and vegetables . . . it's the world's reserve in case of mass destruction.

Almost every country in the world has made a deposit. But only one has made a withdrawal, and that only recently: Syria. The war has so devastated the land that they needed to ask the world's reserve for some seeds to start again.

It fascinated and horrified me at the same time, that a seed bank in case of world destruction would be needed. That we need to have a back-up plan to safeguard ourselves against what we've forgotten—how dependent we are on each other, and the planet.

But I also imagined walking through row after row of all those seeds. The magnitude of all that potential. That mountain vault might as well be holding bars of gold. Seeds are the precursor to currency. They are the original coin. And it felt inescapably hopeful that I stumbled upon this scary and interesting fact.

I resonated with needing to start over, or wanting to begin again. Actually, I didn't want to start over, who does? I just knew that I was at an end.

"Every nature, every modeled form, every creature, exists in and with each other." This is how the Gospel of Mary opens after the initial missing pages, and I am not sure if there was ever a more

eloquent way to describe love. It's not a love we've seen in practice very often. Sometimes, in moments of crisis. But it's a love that renders us all equal. It's a love that says I am not separate from you. We exist in and with each other. It's a love that reaches everything, and everyone. If we all exist in and with each other, then we are all inextricably connected.

There is no stranger, no immigrant, no alien, no other.

I was realizing, as I was wide-awake yet again at 3 A.M., that being fiercely independent only gets us so far. And it's actually a good sign when an old way we're operating in the world comes to an end, but it doesn't feel good. At all. It feels like anxiety attacks, or drinking too much, or insomnia, or watching TV like we'll get paid for it. Or a little bit of all of the above, which was how I was handling it.

Sometimes it has to get worse before it gets better. I like this adage. I cling to it. It's true to the same degree that you can't half-ass death. You have to die all the way to be dead. And this is what scares us about it. Its finality. But in life, this is just the way it is. You have to die all the way before you can resurrect.

So, for me, when things got worse, when I was moving every other year to afford rent, until I found myself isolated out in the woods, which felt like the wilderness after city living in tiny apartments for most of my life, the fourth move with my little man, my seven-year-old son, and I was awake night after night, because being alone in a house unsettled an old trauma, from dormant to a palpable terror. I dreaded going to sleep.

And as much as I tried, I couldn't reason with my nervous system. I would hear a noise while asleep, and I'd shoot up in bed like a meerkat, unable to relax for the rest of the night.

I was exhausted.

I was exhausted not just from a lack of sleep. It was from all the energy it took to remain blind to what I could almost see that night, but not quite. It was standing right behind me like Jason in his hockey mask from *Friday the 13th*. I needed to go "home" to Cleveland. (Cue horror music.) I could afford to stay still then, and I would have family to help me. But then, I would also have to come face-to-face with why I had left home in the first place.

So, now I'll tell you what I heard later that night, after reading about the world's seed bank. Just, don't judge me. Or try not to. Actually, I can't ask you that because I judged it. When I heard it, I felt one of those sinking sensations, as if my whole body responded with "fuck" in slow-mo.

I was lying there in bed, frozen again like a wide-eyed meerkat because I had just heard a loud, very suspicious noise from the basement, and maybe you've had a night like this too, or some version of it. When seemingly beyond your control, your mind starts making a moral inventory of all your shortcomings, of all those times when you now realize you should have said yes, but said no. And the opposite. All those no's! As if there was a way to not end up here. As if there could have been a choice that would have led you to that expectation you had for your life.

Then, for this quick, but clear millisecond, I realized that this state of mind had become my default. I realized I was imprisoned again in this onslaught of judgment. I wasn't actually there in my room, but trapped inside my thoughts. And in that millisecond, I saw all the comments I had been making about myself, about still being single, and isolated, and lonely, and disconnected, and anxious, and literally in the dark; and I realized it was like listening to the comments of a crazy online troll. Every night, I was getting in bed with a poop-emoji-slinging troll, tearing apart where I am right now, and why I'm not where I thought I would be. And that troll was me.

I said a prayer.

And what I mean by prayer is I finally took a breath. I realized how trapped I was; how I had become bound and overrun by what *A Course in Miracles* refers to as "the tiny mad ideas" of the ego. And I got that this is exactly what a "demon" is.

I took that first breath, and let it just anchor me into my heart. *"Every nature, every modeled form, every creature, exists in and with each other."* I felt my love for my son, and let that love, which contains unfaltering forgiveness, extend to me. As I found so often, my love for him teaches me how to love myself, how to let love reach within me where it has never been before.

And then, I took another breath, and I imagined with that second breath that it lit this stubby little candle in my heart. And then I asked, with the minuscule, almost imperceptible amount of space that light carved out, "What the hell do I do now?"

These hot, heavy tears dropped from my eyes, because being that close to what I was actually feeling hurt. And it felt good too. The honesty in it. Then, I heard the answer. But again, I don't want to freak you out. When I say, I "heard" the answer, it's not a voice as if on an intercom at Target, or on an airplane. There's no comparison actually. It's a sound that never reaches the ears, having come from within them. It's a voice that comes from silence. And I know that seems contradictory. But maybe, because you're reading this, you already know what I mean.

So, the third breath I took, I took with my whole body. My lungs filled like gills, billowed out beyond my rib cage, and just shifted the weight of everything, because I heard, within me, in that voice that's more of an experience than a sound, the answer of what's next for me.

"Give to me what you cannot carry."

And maybe that seems really basic. Elemental. But it changed everything for me. And the reason why—the reason it felt like my whole system was responding to that answer with a loud, bold-faced f-u-c-k, in slow-motion—is because as simple as that line sounds, I knew that it meant starting over for me.

"Starting over" isn't it exactly. It's more like becoming aware of what I've always known. It's nearing a closer proximity of what's actually true for me. I guess it's about integrity. In that moment, I understood I had the power to start all over, which just means to recognize what has been true for me for as long as I can remember.

"Give to me what you cannot carry" was asking me to start again, now, with what I've always known, and sensed: that there is so much more here, unseen, that I could be counting on, leaning on,

trusting. That I exist in and with a presence that's in this silence, in this tiny space, with a stubby little candle, here in my heart.

What I mean is (and I'm realizing I'm the one who's freaked out to admit this), *"Give to me what you cannot carry"* came in a voice and a presence I recognized. It's a love that has never left me.

A love that I couldn't seem to either reconcile or reject.

But now I knew I had to. I knew I would have to tell this story—the story of the Christ I've met with because of Mary's gospel. I knew that the only way forward and through, would be to die to who I had thought Christ was, die to what I thought it meant to be Christian, and actually begin to figure out what it means to me.

THE FIRST POWER

DARKNESS

What We Have Forgotten

If I could start over, from the beginning, I would start with the most invisible, the threads in the web of our ecosystem that are rarely named, much less revered. I would start by listing the names of the trees, the flowers, the seeds that carry the light that give us life, because this is what we have forgotten. This is where our reverence has not yet reached.

I would start with frankincense and myrrh, with the Boswellia and Commiphora trees that made them. I would start with the honeybee and the sweet essential nectar it feeds on. I would start first with what goes unnoticed, with what we haven't realized is the most sacred among us.

I would start with the names of everyone we've excluded, of the street children, of the millions slowly starving to death in plain daylight. I would start with the outsiders, the outcasts. I would start with every one of us who thinks we aren't worthy of love just as we are. I would say each of their names, each of our names, who have been made into objects, who have been violated, who have had to survive by leaving the body altogether.

I would list the names of all the mothers who have known the unspeakable joy of gradually knitting life within her, of bringing life from the dark into the light. The mothers who have no idea where their heart is anymore, now that it's also outside of them. The mothers who remind us, no matter who we are, that our first country was a woman's body, and our first element was water, and that our first reality was darkness.

If I could write the beginning, it wouldn't be in the light. It would be in the womb, in the dark, in a cave, in an egg. It would be to name all that has been left out of what's holy. The blood, the body. Nothing real or imagined has ever happened without it.

If I could start again, I would install an altar within me. I would place the most sacred object inside it: my own heart. If I could start again, I would know that the only cathedral I've ever needed to find, to enter, to return to again and again, is this humble red hermitage, this mystical space that holds all the answers. I would begin again inside my heart. And I would live this way. Speaking from it.

If I could start all over, I would begin with her. I would list all of their names first as an introduction, a forgotten lineage: Inanna, Enheduanna, Isis, Quan Yin, Miao Shan, Mother Mary, Sarah-La-Kali, Thecla, Perpetua, Joan of Arc, Marguerite Porete.

I would start with the other, hidden half of the story, the voices that were buried in deserts, and caves, the ones that were burned at the stake. The ones that were so threatening because hearing their voices would mean letting our love reach where it has never been before; to all of us, to all of creation, to the least among us, to the trees and the flowers, to the honeybee that feeds them, to the frankincense and myrrh, to the bark and the dirt, to the land itself where the word was first spoken.

If I could begin again, it would be with her love, because this is what has been forgotten. This is what we need most to remember. That she could hear him, meet him, from within her own heart. That she had so much to teach us—that her love for him taught her. I would start with her love because this was the bridge. This is the bridge. This is how we move the story of what it means to be human forward. We hear from her, we hear from her about what her love made possible.

If I could start again, it would be in the darkness. And in the darkness, all we would see is a hand suddenly extending out toward us. And the invitation would be terrifying. Seeing this hand would compel our heart to start beating, rapidly, audibly. The fear comes from feeling out of control. We want to leave and we want to stay in equal measure. We want to know what might happen next and for everything to remain exactly the same. Taking this hand is a choice to surrender. Surrendering it all. All of the fear. The hurt. The anger. And the ego that created it.

If I could start again, I would start with Mary Magdalene, because she is the one who remembers him. The Christ I know by heart.

The Christianity We Haven't Tried Yet

Then Peter said to him, "You have been explaining every topic to us; tell us one other thing. What is the sin of the world?" The Savior replied, "There is no such thing as sin."

— Mary 3:1–3

I'm not sure what I was expecting when I first went to church as a little girl. Yes, I do. I was expecting the outside to be like the inside. I wanted the great big, unsayable love I felt within me to be seen or witnessed outside of me. Back then before I felt separated from it, there was this wide expanse of love inside me, like my own private ocean.

And so, I guess I was expecting for church to be this place where everyone walks around and greets each other, from one ocean to another, their innermost self, right there on the surface, their inner world rising up from the depths for a breath of fresh air. A place where we can hang our masks at the door, and just help each other be human. A place that reminded me how to be here in this world while not forgetting the part of me that is not of it.

But that wasn't what it was like.

I'm not a Christian. Though I've baptized myself, many times. Like the fiery Turkish prophetess from the 1st century, Thecla, who was denied by Paul when she told him that she was ready to be baptized. She said to him, "Only give me the seal of Christ and no trial will touch me." But he didn't think she was ready. He told her to be patient. Thecla knew her own heart. (Which is why I love her.) And instead, she cut her hair short and baptized herself.

I didn't hear about Thecla until I was a young adult in seminary, where I learned that *The Acts of Paul and Thecla* date back to 70 A.D., which makes it as ancient as any of the gospels in the New Testament. This was the beginning of my education, or my re-education, that what I was searching for was within Christianity but not of it. Thecla wasn't remembered as the first prophetess. Her story didn't set the precedent for the voice of women in the church hierarchy. It was far too filled with a truth we weren't ready for back then. Because for Thecla, salvation was something she found within her.

But more about her later.

The baptisms in my life, which are more accurately just ecstatic skinny-dips, have come as markers when I felt like I was expressing more faithfully what's within me; when I'm no longer denying or silencing this quiet, unassuming voice inside me.

I'm not a Christian. But I find myself having to make that distinction often. Or that I need to make certain no one mistakes me as one. I wasn't raised religious, I was raised feminist.

My great-grandmother, Big Margie (who was tiny but had a presence so large it seemed to enter the room before she did), was a suffragette. She would whisper crazy comments to me when I sat on her lap, like, "It's fine if you want to become a wife and a mother, just make sure you get paid for it."

My mom, Margie, marched for the Civil Rights Act, and for the Equal Rights Amendment, and taught me to protest for women's rights when Roe vs. Wade was in danger of being overturned in the early 1990s. I was 13 and my little sister was just a towheaded three-year-old. Her Planned Parenthood t-shirt came down to her knees.

I was holding her hand when an elderly woman approached me, clutching a pro-life poster with an iron grip. She came right up to me, until we were awkwardly chest-to-chest. She hated me. I felt it. It was visceral. I mean, she hated who she thought I was. She was so angry as she spoke that small beads of spit landed on my face.

She said, "How many will be enough for you?" I had no idea what she was asking me. I wasn't there because I thought I would ever have an abortion myself. I was there because I knew that if anything was holy, it was the relationship between myself and my own body. It was too intimate for anyone outside of me to ever shame or control.

I've always felt I would have to rewrite the history of Christianity to officially become a part of it. No, I would have to turn back the globe like Superman when Lois Lane dies, and make certain they get the message straight from the start. Or the message as I have come to believe in it; that we are not inherently sinful, or unworthy in any way, and that we shouldn't feel shame for how human we are, or how often we break, lose faith, and make wildly misguided mistakes.

When I went to church for the first time as a little girl and read the bible, I broke out in hives. I couldn't reconcile the feminism I had been raised in with the idea that god was a Father, and that salvation only came through his son, Jesus, and therefore men held this exclusive right (being the same sex as the Father) to speak on behalf of him.

The body never lies. And I got a blaringly clear message written in red rashes across my skin that this was a system of belief that doesn't match what exists within me. So, I left the church. Physically. I marched out of the First Unitarian Church of Cleveland. But the turmoil, the anger, as well as the fierce love, and longing—it went right along with me.

I spent my years at seminary searching through the church's history for when women were silenced, for how the Pope happened, and all those male cardinals in red, and why a Popess could not even be imagined.

I searched for the stories and the voices that had been edited out or, in the case of Mary Magdalene's gospel, torn apart and buried.

I remember the first time I led a retreat about the Gospel of Mary and started with this passage, *"There is no such thing as sin."* We were sitting in a circle, so I could see the immediate response—every face lit up with equal amounts of shock and excitement.

There is nothing inherently sinful about being human, I explained. There's nothing sinful about the body, or sex, or sexuality. Being human isn't a punishment, or something we need to endure, or transcend. Being human is the whole point.

We just also don't want to forget, or miss the mark, which is how the word for sin translates from the Greek, by mistaking ourselves (and others) as only this body. We are this body, yes, and all the raging humanity it demands. And also, we are this soul. Both.

One of the women in the circle, Ger, was in tears. I knew from what she had shared during the retreat that she was from Ireland, raised religious, and that she had been sexually abused as a child. The warmth radiating from her made me fall madly in love. I'll never forget that joy beaming out of her eyes, through her tears, like headlights switched to high beams.

And I can't remember if she said this at that retreat or later, when she joined my spiritual community, the REDLADIES, but it struck me because it wasn't what I had intended when I began to talk about Mary's gospel. I just wanted to share and discuss Mary Magdalene's teachings. But she said, "You've reminded me of the Christ I knew before I went to church."

For me, finding Mary Magdalene's voice, her gospel, was like finally attending that church I had imagined church would be like as a little girl, a place where we're not trying to be better than anyone else, or to be better than who we are in that moment. Everyone, no matter who we are, and everything, is included, especially the body.

I'm not a Christian. But I recently came across a quote from the English philosopher and lay theologian G. K. Chesterton that sums up what I have come to believe: "Christianity isn't a failure; it just hasn't been tried yet."

So, I'm not a Christian, or if I am, it's a Christianity that we haven't tried yet, one that includes Mary Magdalene. It's the Christianity that existed before the church. It's the church whose doors are ripped off at the hinges. It's the Christianity that includes all that has been left out.

How a Feminist Sees an Angel

The Savior replied, "There is no such thing as sin; rather you yourselves are what produces sin when you act in accordance with the nature of adultery, which is called 'sin.' For this reason, the Good came among you, pursuing (the good) which belongs to every nature."

— Mary 3:3–5

There's a legend that Mary Magdalene was lifted up seven times a day by the angels. She lived in a cave in the South of France, where she had escaped persecution after her brother Lazarus was beheaded farther south in Marseilles. Supposedly, she had been preaching, ministering there in France in the years following Christ's crucifixion. And in the last 30 years of her life, she remained in this cave, known as La Sainte Baume, where angels gathered her up and transported her to the peaks of the mountain range, to the rarefied air where their messages could be heard more clearly.

In the artistic depictions of this legend, Mary Magdalene is held literally, physically, by a bevy of angels. Wings surround her body, and her hands are pressed to her heart with her gaze directed even farther upward. For example, in Italian Renaissance artist Giotto di Bondone's painting of this legend, Mary Magdalene's body is covered only by her long red hair and lifted up by four angels, her hands pressed together in prayer.

I think Mary *was* lifted seven times a day by the angels. But I also think we've deeply misunderstood what this scene represents. If we can find our way back to this legend in Mary Magdalene's story, seeing with a new sense, perceiving with the eye of heart, we'll remember a truth so many of us have forgotten.

We'll remember that this scene isn't unique to Mary Magdalene. It's the vision of a path that's possible for all of us. We'll remember that this artistic rendering of Mary Magdalene is actually a depiction of an inner transformation, of the very real and formidable terrain we can cross in order to know who we really are. And we'll remember that an angel is simply a thought that lifts us up from out of ourselves, from out of those cages the ego would prefer for us to remain within.

If this is all you read, if you put down this book at the end of this sentence, know that this is the most important message of Mary's gospel: we are inherently good.

Now, if you're still with me, that goodness can never be lost. We can feel lost to it. But it is woven into the fabric of who we are; it's our nature. Goodness. And the word that for me describes this experience, of knowing this inherent goodness, is *soul*.

The word *soul* to me describes that eternal aspect of our being; an aspect that allows us to feel loved, and to experience that we are love. And that our humanity is *not* intrinsically sinful, or shameful. This human body is the soul's chance to be here.

When I see a painting of winged beings decked in Greek togas or naked with golden halos above their heads lifting up Mary Magdalene, I see this as a symbolic depiction of an inner transformation. I see it as an artistic expression of a very intimate moment when Mary chooses love from within her.

These angels lifting her up in so many of these paintings to me are actually meeting her in her heart, taking her from out of the despair, or lack of forgiveness, or the envy that's oppressing her, and bringing her back again to the good, to god. Angels are the thoughts, the memory, the sensation of love. They are whatever comes and shifts us from being lost within ourselves, to seeing again, not with the ego, but with the eye of the heart.

Sin in Mary's gospel is not about a long list of moral or religious laws; it's not about wrong action. Sin is simply forgetting the truth and reality of the soul—and then acting from that forgetful state. The body then, the human body, isn't innately sinful. "Sin" is when we believe we are only this body, these insatiable needs, these desires and fears the ego conjures. "Sin" is an "adultery," or an illegitimate mixing, a mistaking of the ego for the true self, rather than remembering that the true self is the soul.

The soul lives in the silence, the stillness we have to meet with inside us. (Which can make it hard to hear, and to find.) Words are the ego's favorite outfits. Words are how the ego breathes and fuels the flames of thoughts that start replaying inside us from the second we wake up. Our capacity to see the truth that we are sinless, that we are good, has nothing to do with the eyes.

So, why four angels, and why seven times a day?

I think perceiving the good takes practice. And I think we need help getting to that place above the mountains, deep within the heart, that reminds us of what's good. Especially in a world, or within a heart, that has been shattered and has long since fallen apart.

Luke 8:1–3 is the first passage in the New Testament when we hear Mary Magdalene's name. This is the passage I've mentioned that claims she was healed of seven demons. (But that, for me, confirms her mastery of the seven powers she describes in her gospel.)

Pope Gregory's homily 33 with its interpretation of Mary as the prostitute took off like the hottest possible gossip, as we can imagine, and still reigns as truth today. According to Harvard scholar Dr. Karen King, the reason for the popularity of the Pope's view of Mary (and why it has held the collective imagination for nearly two millennia) is because it served the early church fathers: "this fiction solved two problems at once by undermining both the teachings associated with Mary and women's capacity to take on leadership roles."[5]

And this is what's still at stake with the vision of Mary; from the 1st century to the 21st century, women's spiritual authority within the church has been hard won, opposed, or flat-out rejected.

The last time Mary is mentioned in the New Testament is in John 20, when Christ rises from the empty tomb to her, to say her name. She is the one with the eyes that can perceive him.

Hermeneutics. This is a word that changed everything for me in divinity school and seminary. It means, in theology, the lens you use in order to "read" or interpret scripture. The theological term for interpreting scripture is *exegesis*. You use a certain hermeneutical or interpretive lens then every time you translate a piece of scripture. We all do. Pope Gregory did.

When I read scripture, I interpret it with feminist hermeneutics. I am reading the text from the perspective that we are all equally divine, and human.

What do I mean by *feminist*?

There's this quote I came across as a budding teen feminist by poet and self-professed "warrior" Audre Lorde that made this holy fire race through me as I read it: "I am not free while any woman is unfree, even if her shackles are very different from my own." Feminism here isn't real, or without a divisive agenda, unless it refers to all women.

And thanks to Leila Ahmed's seminal work, *The Discourse on the Veil*, I am a feminist who trusts that each woman has her own criterion of what it means to be free. I don't think freedom is uniform and looks the same for everyone. Freedom is personal.

Ahmed explains in the *Veil* that Western feminists were trying to "free" Muslim women from wearing a veil without realizing that actually, for many Muslim women, it provided a freedom that "feminist" women in the West couldn't appreciate. True freedom means having the power to define what being free means in our own lives.

The brilliant sociologist Patricia Hill Collins defines the term *intersectionality*, coined by Kimberle Crenshaw, as the reality that all women are not oppressed equally. There are intersecting factors that increase or decrease the amount of privilege and power a woman experiences depending on, for example, her race, class, economic status, sexuality, education level, and nationality.

Unless my spirituality is intersectional, it's just oppression dressed in light.

A feminist theologian then, for me, means I believe that every human being is equal parts ego and soul (and therefore worthy of the same rights). I believe it would do as much harm to call god mother as it has to call god father for countless centuries. It perpetuates this misunderstanding that any one of us could be greater or less than the other. It feels important to keep expanding our hermeneutics, our vision of what's good, or god, of what's holy, and sacred. Because only then, as the mystic William Blake in *The Marriage of Heaven and Hell* explains, "if the doors of perception were cleansed everything would appear as it is, Infinite."

The Secret Ministry of Currer Bell

The mystery which unites two beings is great;
without it, the world would not exist.

— The Gospel of Philip

Every year. At least once. I read the whole book, all 400 pages of it, to get to the end. The part in *Jane Eyre* when Jane hears Mr. Rochester's voice as if in the wind, as if from within her. At 13, the first year I read it, it was the most electrifying and magical idea. That love somehow gives us access to superhuman powers that defy the laws of space and time.

Jane Eyre was published in 1847 by Currer Bell, a pseudonym Charlotte Brontë used to obscure the fact she was a female author. Brontë's father, Patrick, was an Irish priest and clergyman. As a woman, of course, she couldn't follow in his footsteps. Or, at least, not exactly. The spiritual overtones and commentaries about Christianity are threaded throughout the novel and entirely unveiled. Charlotte seems to have found her way to preach: through her pen.

She helped me realize that not all ministers have a church, and that maybe, women have never really been missing from the pulpit; they just found other mediums and means.

There are so many women who were never ordained or acknowledged as a spiritual authority. Yet there seems to be a higher law that ordains their voices as among the most holy. Listen to the love-drenched words of Sojourner Truth, who stood up at a women's rights convention in 1863 and immortalized her voice because of the truth she dared to share:

"Then that little man in black there [pointing to a priest], he says women can't have as much rights as men, 'cause Christ wasn't a woman! Where did your Christ come from? Where did your Christ come from? From God and a woman! Man had nothing to do with Him."

Jane Eyre was the first book, among many, that I read like scripture. (Because my body, with its hives, couldn't handle the bible.) I realized the would-be female ministers and priests and bishops had been spread out all over, in all genres, and in all places, both sacred and secular. Our spiritual voices were hidden in plain daylight. In print. And in places where our ideas of religion, of Christ, and Mary Magdalene were accepted because we passed them off as fiction.

Let me set the scene. Jane has suffered greatly from the absence of love in her life, for her whole life. Her love, Mr. Rochester, she realizes too late, has a first wife, who lives in the attic as "a madwoman." I believe she suffered far greater. (But that's the subject of another masterpiece, titled, *Wide Sargasso Sea*.)

Jane's parents die of typhus when she's a little girl. So, Jane is raised by her aunt, Mrs. Sarah Reed, who torments Jane by treating her like a burden, and by loving her own three children in front of Jane, yet refusing to extend that love to her as well. Jane's only consolation is in her love for books.

The day arrives, however, when Jane is fed up. Her cousin John has hit her and belittled her to the point of humiliation one too many times. He strikes her hard enough that she is thrown to the ground. Jane snaps and sets on John like a wild, feral monkey. Bloody nosed, and crying, John tells Mrs. Reed. And with disgust, Mrs. Reed orders that Jane be locked in the Red Room. This is the room where her uncle had died. Jane bangs her fists against the door and begs to be released.

The Red Room is where she finally expresses all her rage and anger for being so mistreated and so misunderstood. She screams, and cries, and eventually becomes so upset she passes out.

Her aunt sends her off to Lowood, a harsh boarding school for orphans run by the sinister Mr. Brocklehurst, who humiliates Jane on her first day by forcing her to stand on her chair with a sign around her neck that reads, "Liar." The only little girl to offer her a smile, and later, a piece of bread, is the redheaded Helen Burns. This one gesture is their communion. It seems small, but for Jane it's a feast, to finally have a real friend. Helen teaches Jane that there is "an invisible world," "a kingdom of spirits," all around them. And when Helen finds herself at the mercy of Mr. Brocklehurst's "Christian" ethics of shame and mortification, by demanding that Helen's gorgeous red hair be sheared off, Jane is there to offer her the same true love and companionship. She cuts her hair off in solidarity with her.

Fast forward to Jane hired as a governess at Thornfield Hall, and for the first time in her life she knows love. She has met her match in Mr. Rochester, the one who treats her as his equal. They fall madly in love. And then comes the separation. The fire. The "madwoman in the attic" is revealed dramatically at the wedding as Mr. Rochester's wife.

Jane is saved by St. John, and his two sisters, who are the opposite of the brother and sisters she was tormented by while growing up. They nurse her back to health after she arrives at their doorstep soaking wet and wordless from a broken heart and a nervous breakdown.

And whereas her cousin John beat her and never showed her kindness, her redemptive "brother" St. John, a minister, wants to provide her with a new life, a life of service. After some time together, he asks her to go to India with him on a Christian mission. He wants to marry her. Jane considers the mission but refuses to marry. And this is when it happens.

Jane hears Mr. Rochester. And I've always considered it significant that it starts with her heart. It all starts with her attention being drawn to it.

It begins to beat quickly, to the point that she can suddenly hear it throbbing, loudly. Then Jane says her heart went still, as if expecting something thrilling to pass through it, like an electric shock. Jane describes, "Eye and ear waited while the flesh quivered on my bones."

"Jane, Jane, Jane." This is what she hears, but she doesn't know where the voice came from. She only knows that this voice is the one and only voice she has longed to hear most.

She calls out to Mr. Rochester to wait for her. And she immediately goes to her room to pray. Not in the way that St. John prays, Charlotte Brontë, or Currer Bell, relates, but in a way that's all her own and just as effective.

And because of this moment, this mystical connection they share, Jane returns to Mr. Rochester. He confirms for her that he had called out her name, three times, just as she had heard.

When the Gospel of Philip says, "The mystery which unites two beings is great," this is the scene I think of from *Jane Eyre*. It's a mystery how Jane hears him, at such a distance, from seemingly within her. How can she be so far from him and at the same time never have left him at all?

And it makes me think of Christ and Mary. That we've underestimated the mystery that unites them. That we've been witnessing it in ourselves and others all along. That we've slowly been acquiring a vision that can perceive just how sacred human love is, and how world saving it can become. Maybe this was the secret ministry of Currer Bell.

Leviticus in Bunny Slippers

Jesus said, "When you make the two into one,
you will become children of humanity,
and when you say, 'Mountain, move from here!' it will move."

— The Gospel of Thomas

Mrs. Van Klompenburg shuffled around the house in a muumuu and pink bunny slippers. She spoke in a whisper as she pointed out the kitchen and the backyard with its odd rock gardens, and then our bedrooms. My friend Shana was given her son's old room. It smelled faintly of gym socks, and it had dark blue walls with a tiny, sad single bed. I got the immediate creeps. And from the look on Shana's face, she did too.

I was given her daughter's old room, which was all the way down the beige, shag-carpeted hall. It had a big window that faced the red rock mesas in the distance and a soft pink comforter on a large double bed. I tried to control my sigh of relief at the sight of it and just smiled back at Mrs. Van Klompenburg, who was already smiling, with an ominous zeal, back at me.

Shana and I were high school seniors taking part in an internship through a nonprofit that allowed us to volunteer on the Navajo Reservation in Gallup, New Mexico. The Van Klompenburgs were our hosts for the summer. We had never lived outside of our secular homes, so the bible reading before dinner completely freaked us out.

Mr. Van Klompenburg had asked his wife to read a passage from Leviticus for us. She stood up on her seat and read with such fervor and excitement about the 76 things that are banned for Christians to do and what the penalty is if they're done. For example, bringing an "unauthorized fire" before God (Leviticus 10:1).

God in this case will "smite you." Or Leviticus 18:22, "Having sex with a man 'as one does with a woman.'" This merits death.

As Mrs. Van Klompenburg stood on her dining room chair in her muumuu and bunny slippers announcing the list of all the do-not-ever-do's for the truly faithful, Shana and I only needed one glance at each other from across the table and we knew Shana was moving into my room.

Every morning, without fail, I would wake to the sound of a small pamphlet being shoved under the door and sliding across the wood floor. The first morning, Shana got out of bed, took one look at it and said, "Jesus Christ."

We were both from an area of East Cleveland with a large Jewish population, so neither of us had been exposed to a "come to Jesus" intervention like this one. The pamphlet was titled, "The Bridge to Jesus." It had a picture on the cover of a woman with her arms up, her face clearly in excruciating pain, apparently from the raging flames all around her. And on the inside of the little missive, it declared that we were sinners; but, rejoice, because we only needed to ask for salvation in claiming Jesus Christ as our Lord; and then we would be saved. Otherwise, it's eternal damnation. It's screaming, and full-on flames.

Message received.

Gordon House was our guide around the Navajo reservation. We were told that he was awaiting a trial for drunk driving and vehicular homicide. We had no idea that Gordon House was a household name at this point in New Mexico. His DUI case would eventually be taken to the Supreme Court. And we had no idea that we would be watching a *Dateline* episode about him when we returned home that next fall. The summer we were with him was the last one Gordon House had on the reservation before being sentenced to 22 years in jail.

The fatal crash had happened on Christmas Eve. He testified that he drank seven beers that night but that his confusion was from a migraine, not the alcohol. He had a documented history of migraines and was treated with traditional Navajo medicine; he was on his way to the medicine men. He thought he was on the access road, which runs parallel to and in the opposite direction of the interstate. He wasn't, though, and he hit a car carrying a family of Christian missionaries head on. The impact killed a mother and her three young daughters.

Gordon House was the first in his family to have a master's degree. He was an Air Force veteran and had been a social worker for the Navajo Nation. At the time of the accident, he was the director of The House of Hope, which offered substance abuse counseling to Navajo teenagers. He was deeply respected in his community. And his pride in the Navajo people was palpable.

Our days in Gallup, New Mexico, looked something like this: in the mornings, Shana and I would be reminded of the eternal life or eternal damnation that awaited us, and that all hinged on our choice to either repent and come to Jesus, or continue to live our lives in sin.

A little eggs and bacon on the side.

And then, we would volunteer at the adolescent shelter for Navajo children whose parents or caregivers were in rehab for substance abuse. The kids called us "bilagaana." It sounded like it would translate into English as something like "pretty girl." Gordon informed me, with a slight smile, that my translation was incorrect. We were being called "white girl." Shana and I as volunteers would mostly just listen to the children tell stories. Their imaginations were so vibrant. When I mentioned this to Gordon, he explained, "There is no word for imagination in Navajo." A dream, or what we can imagine, holds equal weight to what happens in "real life."

After work, Gordon would pick us up at the Van Klompenburgs' and immerse us in Navajo culture. He took us to places that the Navajo consider sacred, and to the sites of horrific battles where the Navajo lost their fight to save their land from the American people. And he told us about the stolen generations of Navajo children taken from their families to go to government-funded Christian boarding schools where they weren't allowed to speak their own language, where they were abused and taught to be ashamed of who they are.

Gordon let us participate in a ceremonial sweat lodge and a traditional rain dance. And there was something about being in a sacred circle that taught me the most essential spiritual truth.

There is no hierarchy in the spiritual world.

The people I sat in a circle with in the sweat lodge, chanted with, lit sage with, cried with, and sweated for hours and hours with, and the people I danced in a circle with in the rain dance, called out to the ancestors with, and praised the earth together with the soles of our feet, were all strangers, and different from me. Yet they were strangers that moved me to tears, strangers I loved as I stole glances at them in the heat of the sweat lodge, in the sobering cold of the rain dance, because they reminded me of what I had forgotten: we're all connected.

There is no hierarchy in the spiritual world. There's just this circle where the first becomes the last, and the last becomes the first.

"When you make the two into one"—that line from the Gospel of Thomas means to me that when you're no longer separating yourself from anyone else, when you're not making yourself (in the constant ticker tape of ideas that stream through the mind) out to be better or, more often, worse than anyone else, then you're able to see the ultimate connection that exists between us.

"When you make the two into one" to me describes an internal state that affects every external relationship. When you make the ego and soul into one, you can no longer divide yourself from others. And this is what moves "mountains," or deeply held, almost immovable beliefs: we unify ourselves with love.

The Van Klompenburgs drove us to the airport in Albuquerque at the end of our stay. It was the longest two hours of my young life. I can still see the ardent look of anxiety and fear on Mrs. Van Klompenburg's face as she begged us from the front seat to repent. Her typical fervor for Jesus was even more amped up because of her mistaken idea that Shana and I were sleeping together for romantic reasons rather than the fact that we were just terrified of her.

I wanted to tell her what I felt burning inside me to say since that first pamphlet was shoved under our bedroom door. I felt a raw, terrifying anger in witnessing the hypocrisy of a religion that sees itself so far above and set apart from others, it can justify genocide. But it felt like I might morph into a dragon if I opened my mouth, and I wasn't sure when or if I'd morph back. It was a rage that I didn't know how to express yet without feeling like I'd be consumed by it.

I never said a word to her. But it felt like this tiny, truest part of me was yelling at Mrs. Van Klompenburg and her Jesus from the back seat. It felt like I could hear this hot molten lava core of what I ardently believed with an evangelical fervor equal to hers. It felt like I matched her level of crazy with my own. And it sounded something like this:

I feel sorry for you. That your god is so small. That your god has such a fragile ego, he'll send us all to hell if we don't believe in him. And that your Jesus only loves his own followers, people who have surrendered over everything to him, like some power-hungry, twisted cult leader. I think you've missed the whole point. You've mistaken god for power. I think whoever the hell Jesus was, he was about love. I think Jesus was about a love that's the opposite of power.

THE SECOND POWER
CRAVING

The Girl Who Baptized Herself

In the tumultuous time immediately after Christ's crucifixion, Christianity is seen as a forbidden religion. It's illegal to be Christian. Yet, this crazy, devoted man named Paul is traveling, from village to village, telling stories about his experience of Christ. He happens to stop in a small village where a 17-year-old named Thecla lives. She can hear Paul from her bedroom window. And she's riveted. She remains at her window for three days and three nights as Paul recounts his misadventures with Christ.

Something begins to unravel for her. Or something that had always existed within her suddenly races to the surface, and in those three days her life is transformed. Her fiancé begs her to come away from the window. He tells her that she should be ashamed for directing her love away from him. He reminds her of her duty, of the law. And he enlists her mother, who begs for her to return to them as well. But Thecla remains. And even more, she begins to want to meet Paul and to leave the life that had been expected of her for a life she now feels is authentically her own.

Her fiancé reports Paul to the governor, calling him a magician, attributing him with the powers to persuade young women not to marry. The governor has Paul arrested and sent to jail.

Thecla leaves her house in the middle of the night to go see him. She gives her bracelets to the prison gatekeeper as admission, and he lets her in. She gives an ornate mirror to the guard at the cell door, easily discarding the remnants of her old life. He lets her in as well. Then she goes to Paul and sits at his feet.

The next day, word gets out that Thecla had been to the prison to see Paul. Her fiancé is beyond outrage. Thecla is his! She is his possession. Thecla's mother agrees and screams for her punishment. Her own mother suggests that she is burned at the stake for breaking the law of her betrothal, for going her own way, for following her fiery, young heart.

The governor has Paul whipped and thrown out of town. But to teach a lesson, he has Thecla stripped and binds her body to the stake.

The pyre is lit. And I've always imagined that she was visibly trembling. But that her resolve comes from a place within her, and it gives her this courage that reminds her of who she is, of what she's capable of. Just as the flames are beginning to reach her, Thecla makes the sign of the cross and a sudden thundercloud covers her and all the spectators. Rain pours down onto the fire that was meant to take her life. And she is saved. She has saved herself.

Thecla finds a robe to wear, a robe that was more commonly worn by men, and sets off in Paul's footsteps to catch up with him. A child finds her in the market of a nearby town, a child who knows where Paul can be found.

Thecla is led back to where he had been waiting for her, in deep prayer, not knowing if she had lived or died. She greets him and informs him that she will cut her hair and follow him wherever he is led. He's flattered, I'm sure, but also concerned. Thecla, it seems, was extraordinarily beautiful. So, he voices his fears that Thecla will only run into more trials as an unmarried young woman in this forbidden religion called Christianity.

She reassures him, "Only give me the seal of Christ and no trial will touch me." She wanted baptism, she wanted confirmation from him, her elder, that she was ready and even maybe worthy of being baptized. Paul responds, "Be patient." So she listens, as patiently as love does. And she remains with him at his side.

Their ministry leads them to Antioch (an area that the Romans referred to as Asia Minor, which was an epic portion of the entire Mediterranean). They are walking down the crowded streets in the center of town when the president of Syria, Alexander, notices Thecla and decides he must have her. Right there, as his own. First, he pleads with Paul and offers him bribes of money and power, hoping to appeal to Paul's greed. Paul pretends that he doesn't know Thecla. He essentially disowns Thecla right there for everyone to see. She yells out, wise and empowered teen that she is, and insists that Alexander not violate her.

Alexander, being a president rife with power, goes for it anyway, and tries to take her right there in the street. Thecla won't have it. She rips his crown from his head and tears his garments, drawing attention to his actions and, subsequently, shame from onlookers. Again, Thecla is saved. She has saved herself.

She's brought before a court to judge her actions and is sentenced to death in the stadium. Thecla, again, is stripped and her hands are bound. She's led out into the stadium to face her fate. She is forced to wear one word, which is the word that encapsulates how she has been charged: *sacrilege*. She is wearing the word *sacrilege*, standing naked in the center of a packed stadium as the crowd cheers on the arrival of the wild beasts that are meant to take her down.

A ferocious lion approaches her. I've often imagined the look of love she must have given it. Courage coming face-to-face with courage; the depth of recognition that must have been there. Supposedly, the lioness stopped charging at Thecla and instead lay down at her feet.

Frustrated, the officials send out more wild animals to attack her, but the lioness has now become Thecla's protectress. And she mauls each next beast that tries to harm her. Eventually, the lioness is killed. But the crowd has begun to turn.

The women in the crowd begin to scream, "Unholy judgment." They start to proclaim Thecla's innocence and to voice the true sacrilege, which is to put such love to death.

In the stadium with Thecla is a pit of water filled with wild sea lions. As more beasts enter the stadium and charge at her, Thecla declares, "In the name of Jesus Christ I baptize myself." As she enters the water, a cloud of fire suddenly surrounds her so that she can't be touched. And for a third and final time, Thecla saves herself.

The women in the crowd now recognize who she is, or maybe they recognize themselves in her. This is the part in her story that I love the most. It's the part that gives me the most hope—when the women in the crowd no longer see her as separate from them. And so, they refuse to let her be harmed.

Together they throw rose petals, nard, cinnamon, and cardamom into the arena below where she is standing. And the intoxicating perfume that the roses and spices create lulls the beasts into a stupor, and they all lie down and fall asleep.

Then the scripture reads, "All the women cried out in a loud voice, as if from one mouth," praising Thecla's courage. In saving herself, Thecla has unified the force of love in all the women around her. In freeing herself, she has freed them.

This story comes from one of the earliest Christian scriptures that has ever been found. It's titled *The Acts of Paul and Thecla*. Scholars know that it was widely read because so many copies have been recovered. But in the late 2nd century, an early Christian leader and theologian named Tertullian condemned this scripture because it implied that women had the spiritual authority to lead communities and to baptize.

The scripture ends by relating that Thecla healed many, that her ministry lasted until she died at the ripe old age of 90, and that she's buried supposedly right near Paul.

I think the most threatening aspect of Thecla's story is that she frees herself from any illusions that power resides outside of her.

The Thecla who was to be married off, the Thecla from a prominent family with the weight of her mother's expectations, the girl who was bound by the law to become a wife and held no earthly rights to follow the dictates, the call of something inside her, she died during those three days and nights when she refused to leave her window and the sound of Paul's voice. She began to move of her own volition. She began to go against expectations of a girl, considered the inferior sex in her time. She began to do what her heart was telling her to do. And this was the sacrilege to those in power. That she refused to obey or validate any authority outside of her. Even, and ultimately, Paul's.

She baptized herself because she realized she could. She realized that all along within her she contained the power to save herself.

And so she did.

The Passion of Saint Perpetua

Matter gave birth to a passion which has no Image because it derives from what is contrary to nature. A disturbing confusion then occurred in the whole body. That is why I told you,
"Become content at heart, while also remaining discontent and disobedient; indeed, become contented and agreeable only in the presence of that other Image of nature."
Anyone with two ears capable of hearing should listen!

— **Mary 3:10–14**

Vibia Perpetua had just recently given birth. Her prison guards allowed her to nurse her son while she awaited sentencing. And perhaps because she was a noblewoman from the uppermost class in Roman society, they also allowed her some amenities: a pen, ink, and papyrus. This is how we know so much about her. Her prison diary from 203, later referred to as *The Passion of Saint Perpetua*, is considered one of the earliest Christian writings we have. Its emotion, its beauty, and its bravery articulate the vision of a form of faith more radical than what Christianity would become even a century later.

She was 22 years old. She was a daughter to her father, a wife to her husband, and a mother to her newborn son. But none of these positions as a woman mattered more to her than the truth that she was a Christian, and this is why Perpetua was in prison.

Felicitas, a slave who was eight months pregnant, was imprisoned with her. I've always imagined that they comforted and supported each other, since now, they were no longer separate. They were no longer defined by Roman's strict hierarchical structures as a free woman and a slave. They were sisters, equals. And this is what made them so dangerous.

At this time in ancient Carthage, in Roman-occupied North Africa, at the start of the 3rd century, converting to Christianity was a crime punishable by death. And this was primarily because Christian beliefs turned the Roman structure of power and authority on its head.

Christianity's premise, that we are all equal in the eyes of god, or the Good, in Mary's gospel, leveled the fervently held beliefs in society that were based on sex, race, property, wealth, and citizenship. Women were defined by their social status as daughters, wives, and mothers. And women, no matter their social standing, were considered property with as little rights as a slave.

The emperor could have no other rival, not even god. So, to honor and celebrate Emperor Septimus Severus's birthday, several young catechumens, Christian converts under instruction in their faith before baptism, were rounded up and held captive. The Christians-in-training had two choices: renounce their faith or be thrown into the arena for public execution.

Perpetua's father visited her several times before her sentencing to plead with her to remember her fidelity to him as his daughter, to remember her place in the order of things.

"My father," she explains in her diary, "because of his love for me, wanted to change my mind and shake my resolve."

During one of these visits, she asks him, "Father, do you see this vase here? Could it be called by any other name than what it is?"

"No," he replied.

"Well, neither can I be called by anything other than what I am, a Christian."

When Christ says at the end of this passage, from Mary 3:14, "Anyone with two ears capable of hearing should listen!" he isn't, of course, referring to our actual ears or the capacity to hear sounds. He's referring to an ability to "hear" or understand the message within the words.

This is what I "hear" when I read this passage.

"Matter gave birth to a passion," which for me means the ego. The ego (this passion that matter, our body, gives birth to) has no real image, or identity. Image, here, is what's lasting and eternal. The ego will die when matter dies, so it is contrary to this more unconditional aspect of our self, or soul: our image.

This image, as we'll go deeper into further on in Mary's gospel, resides in the heart. The command, "Become content at heart," is to say, merge with the image, become more identified with the image of the true self rather than the ego, which will pass away when the body does. Remain discontent, and disobedient with the ego, not only our own, but also others. Don't let the rules, projections, and expectations of a society that doesn't see your true image define you. Only become content and agreeable with the image of yourself that's free from the limits of the ego. Only the soul will satisfy you and be able to define the nature of who you really are.

Perpetua never wavered. She had become content at heart. She knew she would never renounce her faith. She prayed, though, for a dream on how to face the fast-approaching date of her sentencing. She writes in her journal of a golden ladder she climbed in a dream that extended up into heaven. The dream had come to her as an answered prayer. At the base of it was a ferocious dragon. And on either side of the ladder, just an inch to the left and right of each rung, there were all kinds of deadly weapons.

She stepped on the dragon's head to climb the ladder and then she ascended carefully to avoid the man-made instruments of combat and war. She made it to heaven in the dream, and this emboldened her as she stood trial and confessed that she was a Christian.

She also had a dream of fighting an Egyptian soldier in the arena. She watched as her body morphed from being female to suddenly being male, naked, and oiled up for battle. She succeeded in this dream as well.

And so, when she was led out into the arena, stripped naked, and standing beside her sister Christian, Felicitas, it is said that she screamed out confidently to the crowd, again and again, "Love one another." Discontent and disobedient until her last breath, to remain content at heart.

Grandma Betty's Lightbulb Eyes

When the Blessed One had said these things, he greeted them all. "Peace be with you!" He said. "Acquire my peace within yourselves!"

— Mary 4:1–2

My grandmother, Elizabeth, who believed in beer and angels in equal measure, was one of the first Christians I ever met. What I mean is, knowing her, hearing what Jesus meant to her, what she heard when she read scripture, helped me understand that it wasn't the bible that terrified me, it was the way it has been interpreted.

She was a presence of love to everyone she encountered, not just to other Christians. She exuded this profound acceptance, this beautiful refusal to ever judge. There was no hidden agenda, no guilt, or coercion when she mentioned a certain passage from scripture, or quoted a psalm.

I woke up early one morning when I was home from college, when I was wracked with insomnia, when the early tremors of a full-blown anxiety disorder were just starting to bloom. I was so profoundly lost. No, that isn't it. I mean, that's the phrase we use for that stage of life, that confusing not-a-kid-and-not-quite-an-adult mess. But it's not what I was really feeling.

I knew exactly who I was. And I knew exactly *what* I had lost. There was a piece of me that felt missing. An elusive, ephemeral, and yet essential piece of me. Without it, I felt like I was watching my life happen. I was witnessing it, but I wasn't really present in it. I was perpetually caught up in my own thoughts. I was locked in the past or feeling dread about the future.

That morning, Grandma Betty was standing by the kitchen window holding a cup of coffee. Her hand shook as she lifted the cup slowly to her lips. She saw me and smiled her quiet, relaxed smile. It was a smile that wasn't forced. It didn't ask me to smile back. It seemed to start from somewhere inside her. As if what I saw on her face was just the tip of the iceberg. She was so serene. So content. And in comparison, I felt like this very tired and very tiny hurricane.

She wasn't alone, not ever. That's what it felt like to me, when I was around her. I felt like I was in the company of way more than just her. As if I was walking in on something, a meeting, a dialogue, a love affair. Even as she stood there by herself in her little flannel nightgown that went clear up to her neck, smiling out at a bleak, depressing, gray December that only Cleveland can muster. She was present to a presence that resided within her, a presence that seemed to never leave her. A presence that filled her with a love that lit up her face, and made her eyes beam as if two candles were blazing behind them.

We'd become pen pals when I left for college, and we continued corresponding years later when I began my first of ultimately three pilgrimages in search of that light she seemed to innately possess. I studied with theologians, Old and New Testament scholars. But somehow for me, Grandma Betty was always the ultimate authority when it came to scripture. I guess because she was living proof that she had read between the lines, or digested the words in a way that had set her free. And many, many of the most acclaimed theologians didn't have Grandma Betty's lightbulb eyes. They didn't possess the peace that inhaled and exhaled through her.

When Christ says, "Acquire my peace within yourselves!" in the Gospel of Mary, I hear this as a directive to focus not on worshipping him but on becoming like him. To not distance him and distinguish him as other than us, but rather see him as an example of who we all have the potential to become. We can acquire his peace within ourselves. Or, at least, Betty proved to me it was possible.

After Grandma Betty passed, my mom gave me one of the many letters she had kept from our correspondences over the years. It was worn at the edges and smelled like her. My handwriting is a close cousin to hieroglyphs. She had read the letter so carefully that she marked all the words she had worked hard to figure out in pencil above my red ink. I sobbed when I saw this. I could feel her soft gaze in the slow, careful attention she gave to my every sentiment. She had been my witness. My secret, extraordinary minister, to help me sort out why I seemed to love Christ and yet cringe so often in church.

What I learned at divinity school, and later, seminary, is that there was a story about Jesus that won out. There was a version of Christ that was created in the 4th century. Emperor Constantine in 313, by a single edict, converted Christianity from this struggling, persecuted, and forbidden religion—the one Perpetua died for—to a state religion redefined by men.

The process of compiling the current version of the bible, the one you would find, say, in the bedside table of a hotel room, was guided by the need for a unified version of Christianity. In the wake of Christ, there were many "Christianities," there were many communities with varying ideas about what or who had just walked the earth. And beyond the metaphysics of what Christ's existence might subsequently mean, there was also the more practical issue of authority. Who would have the authority to tell the story?

A "master story," or a linear story of Jesus, is captured in the canon. However, according to Dr. Karen King, it's poor history: "First of all, the story is incomplete and noticeably slanted. The roles of women, for example, are almost completely submerged from view."[6] In what has become the "master story" that the canon in the bible relates, the male Jesus selects male disciples who pass on the tradition, and authority to male bishops. Yet, King argues, "We know that in the early centuries and throughout Christian history, women played prominent roles as apostles, deacons, preachers, and prophets."[7]

In 325, Constantine called for the Council of Nicaea, where it was decided which scripture would become a part of the canon and which would then become suppressed (and subsequently destroyed).[8] This is also when the church hammered out it's official creed, the Nicene Creed, which goes something like this: "We believe in one God, the Father Almighty, maker of all things visible and invisible. And in one Lord Jesus Christ, the Son of God, begotten of the Father, before all worlds, Light of Light, very God of very God, begotten, not made, being of one substance of the Father, by whom all things were made; who for us men, and for our salvation came down and was incarnate and was made man . . ."

The various scriptures that didn't make the cut to be a part of the canonical bible all had a common theme: the confirmation of the presence of women in Christ's ministry and his exceptional relationship with Mary Magdalene. For example, the Gospels of Thomas and Philip, among others, confirm that there were three who were always with Jesus: Mary, his mother; Mary, her sister; and Mary of Magdala, who was called his companion.[9] One of the most prominent issues that the orthodox church wanted to solve was how to define the role that women would play, especially when it came to apostolic authority: Would women get to be apostles too, and have an equal role in the church?

Aside from funerals and baptisms, the only time of year I went to church after leaving it was to attend the midnight service on Christmas Eve at the First Unitarian Church of Cleveland. This is when my mom would never fail to sob during "Silent Night." They would pass around a box of little white taper candles with tiny paper skirts to catch the wax once they were lit. And then the lights in the sanctuary would be turned off. And we'd slowly, in silence, one by one, light each of our candles by passing the flame around the room from wick to wick.

Grandma Betty would shelter the flame as her candle was being lit and then the tremor in her hand would force her candle's little skirt to work overtime. Wax would fly this way and that. My little sister Elizabeth and I would laugh with thick love in our eyes seeing her struggle to not get little beads of wax on her hand. And when she did, she'd make the sweetest little shocked "oh!" sound.

It's not that the idea of god the father was so upsetting to me, it was that it was so incomplete. God as the father and Jesus as his only son made zero sense. It just felt like one side of a far more inclusive and radical love story. We have the masculine, the male, and the divine; but there is also the feminine, the female, and the human.

Here I was wedged next to my Grandma Betty, a being who had actually, physically "begotten" a son with her own body. A being who radiates and exudes the kind of light these tiny lights can only symbolize. And yet there is no word of her in the story. There's no goddess, no sister, no mother (who births with her actual body in a very human, non-immaculate way). I wonder, and I wonder why more people don't wonder, what god would be if god was also a She? Or even better, what if god was referred to as the love that most profess god actually is?

If we hadn't silenced women and asked them to leave the altar from the start, I wonder what the world would be like now. And I wonder how girls and women would be treated if we would have been able, all along, to hear who Christ was, who Christ is according to women, to mothers, to daughters, to the souls in a human body that can actually create life inside them. Or, to put it another way, I'm excited to see how the world might change once we do.

Over the years, I have kindly, respectfully, with curiosity and also with suppressed rage, asked so many priests, ministers, and pastors (and rabbis and imams), if god is not a man, a human, flesh-and-blood man, why is it theologically accurate to use the masculine, gendered noun *father*?

How is it not irresponsible to refer to god as a he, when we are all—male, female, intersex, transsexual, nonbinary—made equally in the image of the Divine? How can we not see the misleading hierarchy this re-creates every day?

The responses vary when it comes to this deeply held and coveted idea that god is male. There's aversion: "God the father is an expression of protection and love." This is usually given with a glance that makes me feel like a freak: *Why doesn't she feel the fatherly vibes?* There's diversion: "What was your relationship to your father?" And there's deflection: "Well, you know, of course god isn't really a father; god is simply love." And this last one is often said with a condescension, as if *I'm the one* calling god the father and have gotten it all wrong, as if the priest is patting my head. *There, there, silly child. We all say father, but we don't really mean it.*

Here's how I can best explain what it's like for me sitting in the pew when only god the Father is preached. Remember how in the 1980s, we still thought it was okay to smoke on planes? The statistics had already been reported about the harmful effects of smoking, and even secondhand smoke, but there we were picking our seats in the smoking or nonsmoking section.

And here we are in the 21st century rife with all the statistics on the status of women the world over. The statistics of sexual assault, and abuse, and unequal work wages, and lack of opportunity or education, and forced marriage. Here we are in an age of information about the psychological impact on a girl who only ever hears god referred to as male and as the father. Here we are in a world that practices (or reinforces) within its culture what is preached in its places of worship.

This is what it's like for me to sit in a church that's filled with only "god the fathers." It's like sitting in the smoking section of an airplane in the 1980s. Everyone around me thinks we're golden. And I'm sitting there choking on the fumes.

I felt this quixotic mix of rage and devotion, sitting beside Grandma Betty, listening to the congregation sing "Silent Night" slightly off-key, and trying to stomach the constant reference to god as a father, and a father only. I found myself staring at Betty, smiling at her high-pitched "oh!" when the hot wax made it through the paper skirt of her candle, just grateful to be reading the scripture that was glowing right there for me in the creases of her radiant face.

The Angriest Christian I've Ever Met

Be on your guard so that no one deceives you by saying, "Look over here!" or "Look over there!" For the child of true Humanity exists within you. Follow it! Those who search for it will find it.

— **Mary 4:3–7**

He had sandwiched himself between two boards the length of his torso. They were covered with verses from the bible that clearly, in his interpretation, condemned same-sex relationships as sinful. From a distance, I just felt sorry for him. He could barely move. He looked all red and overheated and hurting from carrying around his body-billboards.

And he emanated that kind of lonely sadness that only the truly depressed can emit. I imagined the smell of empty cans of cat food, a scary cross above his bed, and the most terrifying floral pattern on his comforter. He was a small man with a high voice, and I expected to toss a wary yet sympathetic glance his way as I passed. But as I got closer, and his words became more audible, I got offended. And then I felt a blood-curdling rage.

He was calling himself a true Christian, moved by Christ to convert the "sinners" of the world. My women's college was well known as a safe space for the LGBTQ community, and was located in a small town referred to as the lesbian capital of the world. The veins in his neck were bulging. He was screaming about the wretched people, presumably us, who would burn in hell for their sins. I couldn't believe the amount of hate and rage that he contained. Nearing him felt like trying to work my way past a human time bomb.

I've never identified as straight. The poet Adrienne Rich describes sexuality as a continuum rather than a fixed point. This I identify with.

What feels real is that I fall in love with an aspect of a person that can't be seen with the eyes, only sensed. I remember lighting up the first time I heard a woman in one of my retreats describe herself as a "sapiosexual." She was attracted to a person's intellect. So, I borrowed that for a while. But it's not the mind that makes me swoon; it's the heart, the soul of a person. So, maybe I'm a "cardiosexual"? I doubt I would actually ever say that out loud. But for the sake of truth telling here: I fall in love with hearts, with a person's wild (usually broken), open heart.

"Be on your guard so that no one deceives you by saying, 'Look over here!' or 'Look over there!'" This is a crucial passage from Mary's gospel, because it directs us to the source of our own truth "within." And we need to be careful, wary of those who might suggest that they possess a truth we do not. Or that we need to be like them or think like them in order to acquire it for ourselves. We do not need to give away any of our power to anyone, ever.

Let me say that again. We do not need to give away any of our power to anyone, ever.

Because, according to Mary's gospel, we will find "the child of true humanity" if we search for it "within." We don't have to compromise, ever, and settle for an "almost" version of who we are. We do not have to conform to some external truth, some version of what someone else is telling us is better, or more right, more holy, more human. We don't have to fit in. Isn't that the most blessed thing we could ever be told, or could ever *remember*? We don't have to fit in. We don't have to contort who we are in order to fit a mold that was never meant for us.

When I was standing close to angry-billboard-man, listening to him condemn us to hell for being "sinners," I was upset in a way I hadn't felt since I first read the bible as a little girl and broke out in hives. Or since wanting to confront Mrs. Van Klompenburg from the back seat of her car. If I had hackles, they would have been poofed up, sticking straight out as I came face-to-face with him. Or face to chest—he was really small.

I tried to speak to angry-billboard-man and found that my voice was tripping over itself. I could barely manage to say each next word. The weight of knowing how wrong he was and how right I felt made it impossible to speak calmly or even with much chance of comprehension.

In the moment, I could barely stay in my body, much less convince him of why his hate is so *not* Christian. I wanted to say something like, "Christians try to love like Christ, not to hate and judge people." As if I was an expert. But I was too busy having an out-of-body experience. I just screamed that he had no right to condemn us and then I stormed off crying and had a meltdown at campus security.

I was so offended by the fact that he was calling himself a Christian. That he was justifying his homophobia through his faith. And he was so convicted that he was right. It took me months and months to figure out that what really set me off the most about him was the fact that deep down, I was just as convicted about what it means to be a Christian. And it was *nothing* like his version of hell and damnation and the oppressive laundry list of who you have to be (and not have sex with) in order to get saved, and then admitted into some future, distant "kingdom."

I was just as convicted of my vision of Christ as angry-billboard-man. Maybe even more.

I just hadn't found the scripture yet that justified my faith.

The Buddha Tara's Badass Vow

Go then, preach the good news about the Realm. Do not lay down any rule beyond what I determined for you, nor promulgate law like the lawgiver, or else you might be dominated by it.

— Mary 4:8–10

The *Pistis Sophia*, a 3rd-century text discovered in 1773, contains dialogues with the risen Christ and his closest disciples, especially Mary Magdalene, but also including his mother, Mary, and Martha of Bethany, Lazarus's sister. The expression, Pistis Sophia, roughly translates as the Faith of Sophia, or the Faith of Wisdom. Jesus explains who she is by saying, "Son of Man consented with Sophia, his consort, and revealed a great androgynous light. Its male name is designated, 'Saviour, begetter of all things.' Its female name is designated, 'All-begettress Sophia.' Some call her 'Pistis.'"

Right, I know. Not that clear. But what seems evident in this text is that there's a male name and a female name for god, or what's ultimate. There's a begetter of all things, and an all-begettress.

In the Gospel of Philip, found in the 20th century among the Nag Hammadi scriptures in Egypt, it is explicitly confirmed that Mary and Christ had a relationship that distinguished her from the other disciples: "The companion [*koinonos*] of the Son is Miriam of Magdala. The Teacher loved her more than all the disciples; he often kissed her on the mouth."[10]

If Christ could choose a woman, a being of the race just barely considered powerful or worthy enough to exist at all during his lifetime, as his *koinonos*,[11] his spiritual companion, his equal, this was a fundamental shift in what it means to be a man and to be a woman.

In the *Pistis Sophia*, Mary says to Jesus: "My lord, my mind is understanding at all times that I should come forward and give the interpretation of the words which (wisdom) spoke, but I am afraid of Peter, for he threatens me and hates our race."[12]

In the 1st century of the Roman Empire when Christ and Mary lived, the hierarchies of existence were entrenched, as it will continue to be for Thecla, and Perpetua in the 2nd and 3rd centuries. The female sex, the "race" Mary Magdalene belonged to—the race of women—was considered property, more disposable, and less valuable than a man. Men, especially Roman men in power, were seated up there in the highest echelons of the hierarchical structure.

Christ's love for and partnership with Mary Magdalene, virtually a slave in Peter's eyes, the lowest of the lower levels of existence, caused Peter extreme distress, confusion, and threatened his world order. How could Christ love Mary more than him? How could Christ love Mary, a woman, more than him, a man? This was a breach in the structures of power that his own power depended on.

Clearly, the sexes are different physically. The male and female body both internally and externally have organs that are not the same; essential differences for reproduction. What we see, though, when we're looking at a man or a woman is more than just a body. When we're looking at the body, we're also looking at what we ascribe to the male and female body. And that can crowd out the presence of who we are actually encountering.

There's a whole spectrum of existence that goes unseen, then; the wide continuum of trans, and non-gender-conforming identity that is entirely lost if our vision is geared to only see the male and the female. And when we see things this way, when we project all of our acquired, and borrowed, and learned ideas of what it means to be "male" and what it means to be "female," onto someone else, we fall into the most ancient illusion, and we forget the central teaching in Buddhism: form is emptiness and emptiness is form. Meaning, the male and the female form have no intrinsic meanings other than what we ascribe to them.

I had a girl crush in college on the Tibetan Green Tara, a female Buddha, because of a badass vow she makes to put an end to the illusion that a male body or a female body is more powerful or holy than the other. I was taking a course in Buddhism and learning to meditate, which led me to a Buddhist retreat where, oddly enough, I first learned the Christian prayer of the heart.

Tara, in Sanskrit, means "to cross over." She is known as the mother of liberation. She will do anything to help us cross over from suffering to awareness.

I fell in love with her because of the Tara Tantra. In it, Tara incarnates as a king's daughter. She loves spending her days talking spiritual truths with a group of monks. At one point, they become so sincerely impressed with her, and so elevated by what she teaches them, that they tell her they will pray for her to reincarnate as a man so that she could become enlightened.

Tara paused for a moment, looked at them with astonishment, and then howled with laughter. No, she didn't, but when I first read this story that's what I imagined she did.

Realizing the monks are serious and deeply blinded by the illusion that the female body could inhibit enlightenment in any way, Tara then flips the prayer back on them. She vows right then and there to always reincarnate as a female Buddha until *all* beings are freed from the suffering that this illusion perpetuates. Form is emptiness and emptiness is form.

When Christ says, *"Do not lay down any rule beyond what I have determined for you,"* in the Gospel of Mary—a gospel that predates the exclusion of women from positions of power within the church, which happened in the 4th century—perhaps he's referring to the illusion that a person can only be worthy of leading the church if they are born male.

It reminds me of a passage from Margaret Atwood's dystopian novel *A Handmaid's Tale.* Offred is forced to become a Handmaid, which means she must wear red, to symbolize her rank and the fact that she is fertile. Red also because it associates her to sex (and to her sex), though she herself as a Handmaid is forbidden to show passion. The Handmaids are assigned to a Commander and must produce children for him. In the world of Gilead, there are also Econowives, Marthas, and Unwomen, all depending on their usefulness as females to society.

So, in this world, Offred says that she tries to avoid looking down at her body, not out of shame, but because, she explains, "I don't want to look at something that determines me so completely."

The Gospel of Mary wants us to see that we are not just this body. We are also a soul. This human body is the soul's chance to be here. And this human body, whether male or female, or anything in the spectrum between, does not delimit or determine what's possible for us.

Misunderstanding Mr. Mister

Jesus said to them, "When you make the two into one, and when you make the inner like the outer and the outer like the inner, and the upper like the lower, and when you make male and female into a single one, so that the male will not be male nor the female be female, when you make eyes in place of an eye, a hand in place of a hand, a foot in place of a foot, an image in place of an image, then you will enter the Kingdom."

—The Gospel of Thomas

I didn't know what I was receiving, the import of it. How it had set something in motion, like a silent, slow-moving river inside me, that would lead to carving out my own personal Grand Canyon, or illuminating my own private Taj Mahal.

I first heard the prayer of the heart on a silent Buddhist meditation retreat, of all places. This was not long after my clumsy attempt at confronting angry-billboard-man. And it was given to me by a Christian contemplative, the oldest member of our group, who was in her 70s, and who was so shiny and excited about every step of our retreat, even our silent work assignments, like washing the dishes and sweeping the meditation floor.

She was a tiny waif of a thing and yet somehow exuded more energy than the rest of us. I can't remember her name, but let's call her Penny. She was always, even in those ridiculously early morning meditation sessions, radiating light. She shined. I had never really seen someone glow before, but she looked like she had just recently fallen madly, deeply in love.

Penny taught me one afternoon about the prayer of the heart. She said she repeats it inside her all the time to the point that she rarely has to think about it. She said it's like a song that's constantly playing inside her. She can be thinking about other things all throughout the day, but if she drops into her heart, even for just a moment—there it is—still sounding, still circling back from the end to the start again like a lighthouse in the fog.

Penny had this infectious enthusiasm for what's next in life. For inviting it in. For being in the awe and wonder of what new experiences might yet be possible. She had lived in a cave with nuns in Tibet, she had traveled on a barge with her husband along the canals of France, and now she was learning about Vipassana meditation practice at a Buddhist center in Barre, Massachusetts. She wasn't afraid of what's next; she had her arms wide open to it.

And this is why I loved her. This is why I gravitated toward her during breaks, or tiny windows of time when we were permitted to talk.

Penny first said the prayer in Greek, *Kyrie Eleison*. Instantly, I heard the lyrics of the chorus to the Mr. Mister song playing as if on a loudspeaker in my mind, the lyrics about the road that must be traveled, through the dark, in the night, to reach a highway in the light.

She explained that these two words in Greek translate as "Lord, Jesus Christ, son of God, have mercy on me." I started laughing, which was a bizarre response, but let me explain.

For all these years, I had thought Mr. Mister was singing about his girlfriend Kyrie. Kyrie Eleison. It was a song I freaked out over if I heard it come on the radio as a little girl. I would scream from the back of my mom's red Volvo station wagon and beg her to turn it up. Then I'd belt out the words to what I thought was a love story about Mr. Mister and Kyrie Eleison, a mysterious and somewhat elusive woman, I imagined, who he hoped would follow him wherever he went.

I explained to Penny how the Greek had been lost on me for all these years. And then I asked her, out of curiosity, why she prayed to Christ. Because I knew for me, at least, I couldn't imagine begging Christ for mercy. To me it felt like this internalized oppressive idea that a man had to save me, or that I had to be more submissive to be more holy, or that I had to admit some intrinsic aspect of me was lowly, and nearly unforgiveable, so that I had to beg constantly for mercy (to be worthy of it). It felt shitty. And I couldn't understand how this tiny human glow stick of a woman would choose to set this prayer on automatic replay within her.

Penny said that it isn't the words she focuses on, it's how she feels when she repeats them. She said it's like hitting the reset button on her whole idea of herself. She's a woman, a daughter, a wife, a mother, a Christian, and all these identities can at times tie her into a solid knot. The prayer of the heart, she said, brings her back to the truth that she's none of these identities. These are all ideas. Words. Concepts. Expectations. Projections. The prayer of the heart takes her back to the beginning, or to the current of light that weaves through all these changing identities as the one constant among them.

The Three Marys

Love refuses nothing, and takes nothing; it is the highest and vastest freedom. All exists through love.

— The Gospel of Philip

I think that what makes a place sacred is simply the fact that we've been called to it. Lisbeth, the artist I collaborated with for *The Divine Feminine Oracle,* told me the story of a woman named Emma Crawford who moved to the small town of Manitou, Colorado, for a tuberculosis cure in the early 20th century. While there, Emma felt compelled to climb the nearby Red Mountain. Against all medical advice, she climbed the mountain and tied a red handkerchief at the top. She eventually died of TB, but the spirit of her need to climb the mountain became local legend. The mountain was made sacred simply because she had answered its call to climb it.

I remember the considerable strain it seemed to take my roommate in college not to communicate with her facial expressions just how freakish she thought I was as she explained that I had shot up in bed in the middle of the previous night and shouted about a woman with a red cape on the edge of the sea. We weren't friends before my dead-of-the-night declaration anyway, but it just confirmed for her why this had been the case.

I had no idea what my nocturnal self was talking about. In my courses at college, I was merging my women's studies with my passion for world religions. My senior thesis was on the Hindu goddess Kali. And though red is her signature color, she wasn't a cape wearer. So, I wrote it off as the inevitable outbursts of a vivid dreamer, and as solid proof of why I'm meant to live like a hermit in a single dorm room.

A year after graduation, I was standing on the edge of the sea in the South of France in the small fishing village of Saintes-Maries-de-la-Mer. I was on a pilgrimage to sacred sites of the divine feminine, and Saintes-Maries had a church with a crypt for a saint named Sarah. Saint Sarah is known to the Romani people as the Queen of the Outsiders, and is celebrated each May 24 in a festival where four horsemen carry her icon from her shrine in the crypt down to the sea.

There are three main legends that surround Saint Sarah and who she might have been. The first is that she was a generous, and kindhearted noblewoman who lived in the South of France collecting alms for the poor. She had a vision that the female saints present at Christ's crucifixion would arrive on their shores. In approximately the year 42, when the three Marys—Mary Magdalene, Mother Mary, and Mary of Solome—arrived on a "ship without sails," to Saintes-Maries-de-la-Mer, supposedly Saint Sarah was the first to welcome them with open, and apparently prophetic, arms.

The second legend, referred to as "the golden legend," because of the book *The Golden Legend* by Dominican Jacobus Voragine, written in the 13th century, relates that when the three Marys arrived in the 1st century, Sarah had previously been a slave. She was known as "Sarah the Egyptian," and supposedly possessed healing powers connected to the ancient Egyptian goddess Isis.

The third legend is that Sarah is the child of Mary Magdalene and Jesus Christ. She's the reason the three Marys were being persecuted and needed to escape to France. The Marys wanted to protect Sarah from the Romans. Sarah then is understood and considered in this legend as the living holy grail, or as the Sang Royale, the bloodline of the union of Mary and Jesus.

All three legends claim that Mary Magdalene came to the South of France escaping persecution after testifying before the court of Tiberius Caesar as a witness to Christ's crucifixion and resurrection. And that she preached as a minister about what it means to be "a true human being," *anthropos*, in Greek, which translates as someone who is fully human and fully divine.

"Fully divine" might sound strangely unattainable or just flat-out not relatable. But here's how I have come to understand it.

In that region of France, known as the Camargue, there's a cross that's associated with Mary Magdalene. It's called "La Croix de Camargue," the Cross of the Camargue. It's also known as the Guardians Cross.

The cross at the top represents faith, the anchor of the local fishermen at the bottom represents hope, and the heart in the middle represents the love of the three Marys who arrived in the Camargue in the wake of Christ.

This love is the love that changes everything.

It's the love that's described in 1 Corinthians 13, where Paul writes that even if he could speak the language of the angels, but didn't have this love, he would have nothing. Even if he could know every hidden truth, but didn't have this love, he would know nothing.

It's the love that's kind, never envious or conceited. It's the love that expands when truth triumphs. The love that holds all things, can handle and face all things. The love that is ever hopeful and ever patient. It is the love that never fails.

And this is what makes it divine.

1 Cor 13:13 reads, "Faith, hope, and love endure—these three, but the greatest of these is love." What moved me about seeing this cross was the presence of the heart in the center. Because somehow, through the centuries, the focus on love has been obscured and replaced with fear. Just like the story of Mary Magdalene, and her role in the earliest form of Christianity.

She's there as a love that never failed.

I had no idea before arriving that first time in Saintes-Maries-de-la-Mer that it was associated with the legacy of Mary Magdalene. Or at least I didn't know in a conscious way. But as I was listening to the legends of the three Marys the town was named after, staring at the bright, silky red capes of every hue that are placed around Sarah's icon, that dream from college came barreling back to me.

And it wasn't like déjà vu, or a moment of feeling prophetic like Sarah. It was more a feeling like being led to something that gave my life more meaning; or even more, that this *was* the meaning to my life, to find this life that existed for Mary Magdalene after Christ.

When the tour guide told us about the cave north of Saintes-Maries-de-la-Mer called La Sainte Baume, the Holy Cave, where Mary supposedly lived out the last 30 years of her life, my heart started leaping around like an erratic monkey in a cage. The only other time it had behaved so insanely was when I was madly in love.

I knew my monkey-heart was telling me something. As if my body was dog-earing this moment for me. As if it was making sure I didn't miss this glimpse of what's to come. *Her cave,* I could hear my body applaud and scream, *her cave!*

I had always thought of Mary Magdalene's story ending after witnessing the resurrection. But there was a life for her that began again, right there, where I was standing, in the South of France. A place that had called me to it. And there was a love her story contains, that I was there to find. A love that is "the highest and vastest freedom." A love I was prepared to dedicate my life to remember.

The Red Thread

Jesus said, "I am the one who comes from what is undivided."

— The Gospel of Thomas

I still don't know exactly what it means, or better said, I don't know why it means so much. The red thread. I'm wearing it on my left wrist now. I'm not sure if I'll ever take it off. When I look at it there's this echo, like a radio frequency, or like those little bars that light up as my laptop searches for an Internet connection. It radiates. It transmits. And deep down, in this place that exists before words or thoughts, I just know what the red thread ties me to.

In Kabbalah, Jewish mysticism, the red thread is worn on the left wrist because the left side of the body is considered "feminine." It's the receiving side, the side where our anatomical heart beats, and it's worn there both for protection and to honor the feminine, since this is the aspect of our psychic being that allows us to "receive" spirit, or to know and feel that connection.

In Greek mythology, Ariadne, considered both human and divine, and the consort to the Greek god Dionysus, assisted Theseus when he entered the labyrinth to kill the Minotaur by giving him a red thread. He was able to find his way out of the dark maze because of it.

I've also come across a Japanese legend that relates that the red thread has to do with our fate. That we are tied by this red thread to all the people we are destined to meet in order for the soul to evolve. Every encounter, even the most random, was actually already woven for us in a scarlet tapestry before we were born.

The first time I saw the red thread was the last time I met with the shaman. I was doing work with her to recover that piece of myself that felt missing. Though a "piece" doesn't quite cover it; a missing half better describes it. I knew this other half because of a palpable absence I felt. It was more than loneliness. It felt physical. The absence of this other half was like a phantom limb, like an absence so powerful it becomes a presence. It's a presence that's always there, because of the great tall shadow cast by the fact that it isn't.

The shaman taught me how to have a vision. Or, she taught me how to become aware of the fact that the majority of us have them all throughout the day, whether we're aware of it or not. She taught me how to begin to see with a different form of perception by going deeply inward, or *farther up and further in*, as C. S. Lewis describes it in *The Chronicles of Narnia*.

I'm not sure how others travel in visions, and I get it—if you've never had a vision, you're probably already hovering outside your body just from reading this. It seems like a strange concept. But it's actually not strange at all. It's the most natural thing we humans do. We vision. We use our imaginations. What we don't realize, or what we don't really get sometimes, is that what we imagine can actually affect and change us. What we envision with our imagination isn't just our "imagination."

Between 1913 and 1916, Swiss psychologist Carl Jung developed a form of meditation that he referred to as "Active Imagination." This meditation technique served as a bridge between the conscious ego and what Jung described as the personal unconscious and the collective unconscious, which includes wisdom and information that the ego may not even understand.

What's powerful about Active Imagination is that it helps create pathways between what we are consciously aware of and what remains hidden in the unconscious. Jung linked Active Imagination with the process of alchemy, that ancient effort of oneness, or becoming gold. And by gold, I mean, merging with these fragmented or divided parts of the self. Merging the ego and the soul. Alchemy as a process of unifying our sense of self, into a whole. This is what Jung's *The Red Book* is all about.

The shaman taught me how to find the world tree, a spiritual motif in almost all religions. I remember the first time I saw it.

(I mean inwardly, with my eyes closed.) I was walking through a field, within my heart (stay with me) when I saw it in the distance. It took my breath away. It felt so ancient. It felt like the holiest thing in existence. It felt like seeing a part of me, as if these limbs that were reaching up into heaven were a part of my body and the roots that reached down into the underworld were also coursing through my veins. The psyche, of course, can't be seen, but this tree felt like the nearest thing to an image of it.

There's an alchemical dictum that says, "as above, so below." This was the metaphysical truth I felt that I was encountering in seeing this world tree within me. Everything that happened below in the dark was inherently connected to what happened above, in the light.

The shaman had taught me how to set a strong intention each time I had a vision. I had to ask for the help I needed. "This is how spirit works," she had said to me with a smile. "Spirit is ethical. You have to ask in order to receive." She would have me state my intention out loud, which always made me feel self-conscious, because I looked crazy. But I would do it anyway. I trusted her more than I cared about appearing sane.

And once I stopped questioning everything that happened in the vision, once I trusted that what I heard and felt and experienced was real in the sense that it was really the wisdom I needed, then it all came effortlessly to me. My greatest obstacle was believing it could all be this simple; ask for what I need, and receive it from within. Which is also to say, my greatest obstacle was believing that I could ever be that powerful.

The tree was so familiar to me, like a religion that existed before religion; like the original template that all religions are based on. I knew how it worked. Nothing felt foreign to me.

During this last vision that I had with the shaman there supporting me, I pressed my hands to the weathered bark and sensed that I was meant to descend. I followed the roots until it felt as though the air had shifted, like the cabin pressure in a plane changing altitude. I was submerged into what felt like a different realm or consciousness from the one I was in just a moment ago.

I was standing inside a cave. It was cold, that bone cold that creeps under the skin. The walls of the cave were glistening, wet. I heard a dripping noise in the distance. It echoed somewhere deeper down than where I was standing. It made me feel like the cave was endless. As if the cave never stopped descending downward. *Farther up and further in.*

In this vision, I knew that I had reached the underworld. And I had set the intention to meet with the medicine or message that was most aligned for me in that moment. It had to do with my heart. And that piece of me, or that presence, I felt destined and determined to find.

Then, suddenly, I felt this rush of air, the way the breeze catches you off guard when someone at a crowded restaurant opens the door. I turned in the direction that it seemed to come from and this is when he walked in.

And this is when words start to fail me. But I know that if I'm going to tell this story completely, I'll have to try to keep writing, even past where words end, past the point where words seem to lose their meaning.

He walked in and we immediately knew each other. This is the part that's dream-like, though, because, like a dream, it doesn't really make sense. I write "he walked in" and yet I couldn't describe what he looked like physically at all. Because the recognition seemed to take place with a faculty more accurate than eyesight. And "he" didn't seem separate from me.

Then, we wrestled, but not really. (See, dream-like.) All we were doing was looking at each other. But it felt like we were rolling around like deranged ferrets laughing and exploding with light. We kissed but it wasn't like kissing I had ever experienced (in real life). It was like melding together, it was like each kiss was a return to what's true, to the truest thing of all.

It was a joy that had always existed in me. It was the experience of feeling loved. Loved from the inside out. It was a taste, however brief, of what it feels like when I am no longer absent, when no part of me is missing.

As I gave gratitude and began to climb up the roots of the world tree, I knew this experience or vision I just had was the deepest medicine I would ever receive.

I walked through the field and back into the room, back into my seated position in front of the shaman. Before I opened my eyes, she asked me to see if I had brought anything back with me from that vision. With my imagination, or the eye of the heart, I could see that we were both wearing a red thread tied around our wrists.

Emotions flooded me when I saw this. It felt like I was seeing what had always been there, what we had placed on each other's wrist too long ago for the mind to grasp.

We both took a deep breath. I knew the vision was complete. I opened my eyes to see the shaman's gorgeous brown saucer eyes spilling over with light. She stared at me. It felt like my eyeballs were on fire from all the love streaming through them. Then, the shaman burst into tears. And asked, genuinely shocked and upset, "Why didn't you tell me before now?"

I looked at her perplexed, and waited for her to say more. But she didn't. "Tell you what?" I asked her.

"The red thread," she said as she reached across the space between us and took me into her arms. I inhaled.

I forget so much, so many details about the people I love that have come in and out of my life. My memory seems to be purely olfactory. I knew in that moment that if I inhaled deeply enough, I would never forget her. Her long dreadlocks smelled like frankincense and geranium. I can't smell either now without thinking of her. Without seeing those dark brown saucer eyes light up with a presence that isn't entirely of this world.

I knew not to ask her why the red thread meant so much to her. I pretended to understand, even though I didn't entirely. I knew I would have to live into the reason why the red thread signaled something to her about who I am. About who we are.

"I remember you," she said with more love in her voice than I could even bear. "I remember you."

THE THIRD POWER

IGNORANCE

What Happens in the Wilderness

This is what I learn as a little girl; I am only safe when I am divided.

I learn that there are forces, illusions, deep-seated misunderstandings, ego-driven needs that can overpower me. They come one night in the form of a teenaged boy mistaking me for an object.

And I learn that I have the ability to leave, in any moment, in any situation. I can choose to exist somewhere else so entirely that nothing at all is even felt. I just witness. I see her hands (my hands) frozen in shock. I just watch with eyes now that are as old as the soul that once inhabited my body.

In Aramaic, the language that Christ spoke, the word *death* means "existing elsewhere."

I learn that once that pathway out of myself, and out of the present moment, is created, it's very hard not to choose it again whenever I feel anxious, afraid, or just out of control. I learn to exist elsewhere.

As a teenager, I didn't have the words—I had never even heard the words—to describe what actually happened for me in assault.

That the trauma (of being separated or divided from the soul) can't be seen.

Jungian analyst Clarissa Pinkolas Estes's *Women Who Run with the Wolves* became my bible. These stories spoke a language that I inherently understood, a language of myth and metaphor. I felt this sense of a tribe for the first time in my life. Or a lineage. I felt like my story was the continuation of a story that has been told for thousands of years. I felt I was accompanied always by legions of us, generation after generation of women, healing this ancient misunderstanding that the female body signifies the lesser sex, a being to be owned, dominated, and not trusted.

The tale of the Handless Maiden was my book of Revelation. It was originally collected by the Brothers Grimm in 1812, but existed for an unknown amount of time before that. It starts with a devil, a "demon," a force that seeks to divide the maiden first from her body, then her father's home, and finally from her love, the king.

The devil tricks the maiden's father into giving her to him in exchange for great wealth. In three years, he warns, he will return and claim her. She lives in prayer for those three years and on the day when the devil comes to take her, she draws a white circle around her with chalk. He cannot touch her; her heart is too pure. The devil tells her father to keep water away from her so she cannot wash. He will claim her the next morning when her hands are dirty. The maiden's tears keep her hands clean. And again, the devil cannot claim her.

He orders the maiden's father to chop off her hands. Her father hesitates, but the devil says he will take him instead if he doesn't do it. Her father begs for her forgiveness, and in his fear and ignorance, he does it; he cuts off her hands. The maiden cries all night. And in the morning, for a third time the devil cannot take her, because her tears have purified her soul.

The maiden's father wants to take care of her now that he is wealthy and she is maimed. But she realizes that she has to leave. She can't stay in her father's house. She is no longer safe, or at home. She begins to wander. And eventually, she finds her way into a garden. She rests near a pear tree and meets a king. He's a good king, a kind man. And he loves her, stumps and all.

Out of his love for her, he makes her silver hands. She loves him. They get married. And soon, she is pregnant. But then the king is called away to war. And in his absence the Handless Maiden gives birth to their son. He is beautiful and she adores him. A message is sent to the king to tell him the good news.

But the devil is back again, and intercepts the message and distorts it so that it says that the baby was born misshapen and ill, a changeling. The king is heartbroken to hear about his suffering child but loves him all the greater. And when he sends a response telling the Handless Maiden that his love will never waver, again the devil interferes with the truth, and changes the king's message to read that he wants the queen and the changeling killed.

The king's mother cannot follow through with these orders. So, she straps the baby boy onto the Handless Maiden's back and tells her to run for it. The Handless Maiden begins wandering again. She makes her way eventually to a forest. And there she meets with an angel who guides her to a cabin with a sign on the door that reads, "Here anyone can live free."

The Handless Maiden raises her beautiful boy there in the wilderness for seven years. And in one version of the story, her hands simply grow back through the grace of her love for god. In another, her hands grow back when her son falls from her back into a stream and is drowning. When she reaches her stumps into the river to save him, her hands immediately appear. Either way, her silver hands are no longer needed. Love has regrown her reason for being here. Love has healed her body. And it's not a love that came from her father, or her husband, not even her son. It's a love that came from within her, a love that had protected her and guided her all along.

Then the king returns from war to find that his message of love had been tampered with and that the Handless Maiden, his queen, and his son had to leave the castle for their own safety. He vows to wander the earth until he finds them. An angel leads him to their cabin in the forest. And at first the king doesn't recognize the queen, because she's no longer handless. Then she shows him the silver hands he had made her long ago when they first met. And his face lights up with recognition. They return to the castle, restored to each other, and never to be parted again.

The seven years spent in the wilderness, in a cabin: this is when she becomes whole again. Because as sweet as the silver hands were, they were never going to cut it. Being held in love by the king, being taken care of, was the beginning of something new for her. The birth of her son asked her to leave home again. To go deeper. To not just cover up that horrific trauma with silver, with making do, but to heal all the way through. To no longer carry the scars, the proof of the trauma, around with her wherever she went. To heal to such an extent that her own hands grew back. To reach a love within her that's divine, that upgrades her silver to what's golden and everlasting. To become whole again is to remember that she's undivided.

We often think of the end, the happily ever after, as the external union or outward marriage. To be held in love by another is just the start.

It's not the end. The culmination is when that trauma or wound has left the body altogether, so we no longer have to.

This was the ending I wanted. The end when I have found the cabin deep inside my body with a sign on its door that reads, "Here anyone can live free."

The Gospel of Mary Magdalene

Then Mary stood up and greeted them; she tenderly kissed them all and said, "Brothers and sisters, do not weep, do not be distressed nor be in doubt. For his grace will be with you sheltering you. Rather we should praise his greatness, for he has united us and made us true Human beings."

— MARY 5:4–8

I read scholar and priest Jean-Yves Leloup's translation of Mary's gospel before Dr. Karen King's translation, the summer before entering seminary. I remember seeing it from across the bookstore. I sort of hurtled toward it as if no longer in control of my legs, as if the Gospel of Mary was magnetized and there was no resisting its attraction. I probably looked possessed.

The moment I had it in my hands, I stared at the image on its cover of Giotto di Bondone's painting with Mary Magdalene being lifted by four angels, and then I just sank down and sat on the ground right there and started reading it. I didn't move until I had read the entire book.

I started crying just a couple pages in, when Peter calls Mary his sister. He says that he knows Christ loved her more than all other women. He asks her to tell them, the other disciples, what Christ told her that he didn't reveal to them. And then Mary responds by saying, "I will teach you about what is hidden from you."

Her gospel, her vision of Christ, has been buried for so long. And yet, in that moment, the reason I cried was because her voice felt like a validation. As if somehow my entire life already included this scripture as its rule, as the truth I compared all else to. But now I was holding it in my hands, not just in my imagination, and in my heart as an ideal. Her gospel was scriptural evidence of what I already believed in.

As we move our way through each passage in Mary's gospel in this book, I also want you to have an overview, a Cliffs Notes version, of her entire gospel.

God is not referred to as the Father (or the Mother) in the Gospel of Mary, but simply as The Good.

Sin is not inherent to being human; we are not born sinful. Christ says in Mary 3:3, "There is no such thing as sin." Sin is not some state of being that must be redeemed. Sin is something we produce within ourselves when we misunderstand the truth of who we are; when we forget that we are not just human, we are not just this ego assailed with constant needs and desires. We are not just this body, but also the soul that inhabits it while we're alive. Sin comes from forgetting, and is remedied by simply remembering that messy truth that we are both a soul and an ego.

The gospel stresses the importance of integration. It's not sin but ignorance of our true nature that creates suffering. We have a template, an image that arises or exists beyond this realm and yet seeks its full expression here. Our work is to reunite with that template, with our own angel.

This is Mary's emphasis in Mary 5:8, ". . . for he has united us and made us true human beings."

In Jean-Yves Leloup's translation of her gospel, he mentions *Talking with Angels*, the amazing account of a group of friends in World War II Hungary who each receive messages from their own angel. The only one among them to survive the war is Gitta. Leloup relates the passage when one of the angels reminds Gitta and her friends, "You yourself are the bridge."[13]

We are incomplete without remembering this other half of what it means to be human. To be a "true human being" is to unite the ego, or self, with the nous, or the soul. *Anthropos*, a true human, Leloup explains, comes into being when we complete the connection that exists between the created world (matter, plants, animals) and the creating world (angel, archangel, light itself). The human is in the middle. So, being human is a privilege and a purpose itself. To be the bridge between the created world and the creating world. To be the voice of love for the voiceless.

Mary Magdalene stresses in her gospel that Christ has united us and made us "true human beings." This is why we should praise his greatness, because he has "united us" by showing us the way, by becoming unified himself.

We are capable of integrating the self and the soul, the image and the analogue, the human aspect of us with the eternal self that never changes, what Jung referred to as personality 1 and personality 2. We can become *ihidaya*, Aramaic for "undivided." And this is the ultimate goal. Not a distant salvation, given to us through repentance, or guilt and shame. Or Hail Marys.

We realize this aspect of who we are, our divinity, our angelic form, the nous, or the highest aspect of the soul, by allowing the soul to ascend. This ascension, however, is not about going up and over; it's not about transcendence. This ascension is about going inward, more fully into our own emotions, our own embodiment, to purify the heart.

There are seven powers, as I mentioned at the start of this book, or seven "climates," as Episcopal priest and scholar Cynthia Bourgeault describes them. We need to go through these seven powers and no longer be bound by them in order to attain the vision that's possible, that's actually our inheritance in being human from within the heart. These powers or climates are: darkness, craving, ignorance, longing for death, enslavement to the physical body, the false peace of the flesh, and the compulsion of rage.

The soul ascends because it does not seek to judge, nor does it attempt to dominate anything or anyone. And the soul cannot actually be harmed because it does not belong to the world of the flesh. We are here to attain the freedom the soul remembers. We do this by using the spiritual technique that Christ used called *kenosis*, the path of self-emptying love. It's a spiritual practice that allows us to upgrade from the ego, or the "egoic operating system," as Bourgeault refers to it, of viewing others as separate from us, to the unitive consciousness of the soul.

Christ led Mary through this process of transformation, this spiritual path of integration, this goal of becoming undivided, and this is why she is able to receive a vision of Christ from within her heart. Her self and soul are one; she has become a "true human being." And she can now teach what the other disciples never learned; she can be the apostle to the apostles as Christ's most beloved companion who mastered the vision Christ attained. Mary is able to step into Christ's ministry as the one who acquired his same peace. The one who is connected from within her heart to the same love that Christ made incarnate.

At the end of Mary's gospel, the disciples are upset with this revelation, with the teachings that Christ gave to Mary and not to them. They argue, and express both contempt and disbelief that Christ could reveal such powerful teachings to Mary, a woman, and not to them. Peter is especially peeved. But one among them, Levi, comes to Mary's defense, and suggests that if Christ considered her worthy, then who are they to disregard her? Because, he adds, Christ knew her completely and loved her steadfastly.

Mary's gospel tells the story of a very different criterion for spiritual authority.

Souls are not sexed. So, the sexuality, sex, and gender ascribed to the body are ultimately illusory. These differences are part of the material world, not the eternal world.

We are all souls that cannot be defined by our physical form. Spiritual authority cannot be determined by a person's sex, gender, or sexuality but rather by the depth of their spiritual transformation and subsequent wholeness. Meaning, a person attains the spiritual authority to speak about Christ, or to proclaim the "good" news, not because of what they look like externally but because of how arduously they have worked internally at uniting the self with the soul.

The imperative in Mary's gospel is to become "the child of true humanity," which means fully human and fully divine. It means becoming fully conscious of the eternal, unbounded soul while here in this tethered, limited human form. And this translates to me as trying (and faltering) and trying again to cultivate this love inside us. It means doing all we can to be the presence of love.

Jean-Yves Leloup describes the emergence of these repressed, apocryphal (meaning hidden or secret) texts, like the Gospel of Mary Magdalene, and the Gospels of Thomas and Philip, as an effort of integration, of making the subconscious conscious. We have been very aware of the masculine, linear, more rational story of Christ, but what we haven't heard, what has been hidden from us, and what we haven't been ready to integrate is the equally significant story of Mary Magdalene, of the feminine, of the cyclical, the non-rational, of what waits for us within.

What It Means to Be Saved

When Mary had said these things,
she turned their hearts toward the Good.

— Mary 5:9

In 325 A.D., at the council of Nicaea, church fathers hammered out the creed of the Christian faith, a creed that's repeated to this day in churches all over the world; I've mentioned it before, I know, but it makes sense to chant it again: "We believe in one God, the Father Almighty, Creator of heaven and earth, of all that is, seen and unseen. We believe in one Lord, Jesus Christ, the only Son of God, eternally begotten of the Father, God from God, Light from Light, true God from true God, begotten not made; of the same essence as the Father. Through him all things were made. For us and for our salvation . . ."

To maintain this creed, the four gospels that were chosen for the canon of the New Testament, Matthew, Mark, Luke, and John, needed to have no rivals. So then, all of the gospels that had existed for almost three centuries as scripture sacred to the early Christ movement—like the Gospel of Mary Magdalene, the Gospel of Thomas, the Gospel of Philip, *The Acts of Paul and Thecla, The Thunder, Perfect Mind*—suddenly became a threat to the budding institution of the church. In the year 367, the Bishop of Athanasius of Alexandria ordered that the monks destroy all of the writings not specifically designated as canonical.[14]

But, gratefully, there were many renegade monks (those Copts I could kiss), who disobeyed this edict. Holy rebels. These very wise and industrious monks wanted to preserve the gospels that related a very different Jesus from the one forming within the church hierarchy. Instead of burning and destroying the ancient texts, these mysterious monks buried them in urns in the desert and others deep in a cave. Thanks to the Bishop of Alexandria's order, Egypt became a land of buried treasure.

As you know, the Gospel of Mary Magdalene wasn't among the Nag Hammadi findings or the Dead Sea Scrolls. However, those discoveries help contextualize Mary's gospel and help us understand why all these scriptures were considered dangerous enough to want to destroy.

The similarity between the gospels found in the Nag Hammadi library and the Gospel of Mary, or the common theological thread, is that they all emphasize the importance of remembering Christ within. The Gospel of Thomas, especially, focuses on the effort of transcending the opposites, to become one, single, or *ihidaya*: the unified one.

The path of the ancient Christian was the practice of *anamnesis*, or living remembrance.[15] Christ wasn't understood as a being to follow and idolize, but rather as a master of this path, this transformational process. This path that Christ walked not because he was the only one who could walk it, but for us to see that it could be done. That we could become *ihidaya* as well.

Sophia is the Greek word for wisdom. In the original Aramaic of Jesus and his followers, there was no word for salvation. As Cynthia Bourgeault explains in *The Wisdom Jesus*, "Salvation was understood as a bestowal of life, and to be saved was 'to be made alive.'"[16]

I need to take a minute with this, because that's a revolution in thought. Salvation not as something that's one day given, or earned, by a force outside of me. Salvation as waking up, becoming even more alive. More present. It's revolutionary for me because I see how easily it's missed. If we are waiting for an external source of salvation, we're focused outward. Instead, salvation comes from within. And we achieve this by going inward and participating in a process of remembering the love that's all along just waiting for us to return to it.

With the suppression and disappearance of these early Christian texts deemed "non-canonical," Bourgeault explains that a fundamental shift was established in what theologians refer to as the eschatology, or the ultimate destiny, of humanity. With the creation of the Nicene Creed, there became a heaven to reach in the future, when we die, and a corresponding hell to descend into.

There became a clear need to be redeemed, saved before this death, and this saving could only come through Christ. (And subsequently through the church, and the priests who received the apostolic authority to give blessings and the Eucharist.) This idea of saving became the promise of eternal life. This promise in turn became the soteriology, or the doctrine of salvation, the early church fathers instituted. Our sinful status as humans depended, then, on the church and god's only son, Christ, to bestow mercy and redemption. The doors to heaven now had gatekeepers.

The sacred texts found at Nag Hammadi, along with Mary's gospel, reveal a sophiology rather than a soteriology. They focus not on a process of salvation, but on the *wisdom* of the divine, and on the internal transformation that Christ went through and that we all can go through as well. The Gospel of Thomas and the Gospel of Philip also emphasize the unique and exceptional relationship between Mary Magdalene and Christ, as his *koinonos*, or companion.

If the early church fathers were going to establish male authority, Mary's true identity and relationship with Jesus according to these other "competing" and "conflicting" early sacred texts from the Christ movements in the 1st and 2nd centuries, then Mary Magdalene and her profound gospel would have to be buried, and her identity would have to be retold as someone far less significant to Christ than she was in all of this ancient scripture.

Mary's gospel reveals that she could turn the disciples back toward the good, toward god, which is an indication that she had followed this path that Christ walked to become *ihidaya*. It reveals that she was a leader among other leaders, an apostle to the apostles, and something far more radical and heretical than a prostitute.

What It Means to Be Human

Peter said to Mary, "Sister, we know the Savior loved you more than all other women. Tell us the words of the Savior that you remember, the things which you know that we don't because we haven't heard them."

— MARY 6:1–2

There was far less at stake for me. I could ask questions that they couldn't simply because I was an outsider. An outsider not seeking to ever be let in. I was often asked what I was doing there at Union Theological Seminary, a non-Christian among Christians training to become ministers, reverends, priests. Why would I want to devote three years of my life to the academic and spiritual rigors of divinity school if I never intended on leading a congregation or even becoming a card-carrying member of a church?

I don't remember her name, if I ever knew it at all. Let's call her Barb; that feels about right. What I have seared into memory is the look on her face when she whipped around in her seat in front of me to blast me with one of the hairiest eyeballs in the history of humankind. All because I stated what I thought was the obvious: "If Jesus was fully human, then he must have had sex."

We were studying the fourth Ecumenical Council of Chalcedon in 451 A.D., which established that "Christ is at once perfect (*totus*) in his divinity and perfect (*totus*) in his humanity." So, not half-divine and half-human, 50-50. But rather, fully divine, meaning 100 percent, and also fully human, another 100 percent. Doesn't really make sense mathematically, but it held me rapt with attention. Because it released me from this idea that we were either human or divine. It let me grasp, or at least try to, that we could be both a saint and a screw-up, and that would be perfect; that would be the whole point rather than a contradiction.

The logic for me, before I blurted out the obvious about Christ and sex to the whole class, went like this: if Christ was a "whole" man, as Pope Leo the Great said—*Totus in suis, totus in nostris*—then to depict him as celibate should amount to blasphemy. "How many times will it be necessary to repeat the adage of the early church Fathers," Jean-Yves Leloup laments, "'That which is not lived is not redeemed'?"[17] Or said another way, if there's an aspect of Christ's humanity that wasn't lived, for example, his sexuality, then it was also not transformed, redeemed. "Of course, Jesus Christ lived his sexuality," Leloup exclaims simply, "otherwise he could not have been fully human."[18] And according to the Fourth Ecumenical Council of Chalcedon, attended by about 500 bishops from all over the world, and exactly no women, Christ is both fully human and fully divine.

Mary Magdalene clearly moves among the other disciples as one who has become a child of true humanity, and this is the ultimate goal of her gospel, to become an *anthropos*, a completed human being. The integration of the opposites within oneself. "A child of true humanity," in the Gospel of Mary, according to Bourgeault, is someone who has achieved this state of inner oneness. "It designates the *anthropos*, the fully realized human being: the enlightened master of Eastern tradition, or the monad or 'undivided one' of hermeticism."[19]

The cost of taking Christ's full humanity from him is that the importance, or even the sanctity, of being human has also been stripped from those of us who try to understand his teachings. And the cost of Mary Magdalene's erasure as Christ's partner, or companion, his spiritual equal even, has stripped us of a female model, of how the process of human love can unite us from within.

Jean-Yves Leloup believes that, "The restitution of the true character of Miriam of Magdala as a companion of Yeshua of Nazareth can help men and women today realize their potential of *anthropos*, their full humanity, which is both flesh and spirit, both human and divine."[20]

There were teachings that Mary had "the ears to hear" and that the disciples did not. There were teachings given to her by Christ, in private, and/or from within her heart. Peter and the disciples trust her and ask her to reveal these teachings because they know that Christ loved her more than all other women. He loved her more than anyone else.

But how can that be possible? I imagine Barb asking as she reads this chapter. *How can Christ, if he's god, play favorites? Wouldn't he love everyone equally, as rays of light and all that jazz?*

Yes. And he loved her uniquely among all others. This is radiantly clear. Even if I only ever read the bible, I would have to wonder why or find it curious that Christ rose to her, Mary Magdalene. He let her witness him first. Or, he came back for her. Or, she was there, all along, with him through death, as if from within his heart, as if a red thread tied them together, as if they had prepared for it, and her love tethered him to her, led him through the darkness, to redeem it. And then, his first word was to call out her name, Mary.

He loved everyone equally, yes, as he loved himself. But he also loved her more than all other women. Why? Because, Barb, he was (also) human.

What I Learned as the Burning Bush

Mary responded, "I will teach you about what is hidden from you."

— Mary 6:3

The Greek "Philokalia" was compiled in the 18th century by Macarius of Cornith and Nicodemus of the Holy Mountain. It's a collection of sayings by the Hesychasts. Hesychasm is from the Greek for "stillness, rest, silence, quiet" and is a mystical tradition of meditation and prayer in the Eastern Orthodox Church. This rich, and wacky (I'll explain), contemplative tradition within Christianity had been hidden from me. Up until that point, I had only associated meditation with Buddhism. But Hesychasm is an ancient form of meditation that's native to Christianity, and that has been practiced since at least the 4th century. It just never crossed the divide between the monastic and secular worlds.

The Hesychast would curl forward over his heart, drawing all of his attention and consciousness there, within. The quest for union with the divine was attained by bringing consciousness into the heart. The earliest mention of Hesychasm is in the 4th century with the Cappadocians in modern-day Turkey (or Constantinople), and especially with Evagrius in Egypt in *The Sayings of the Desert Fathers*. Then in the 6th century with Saint John of Sinai, the term is used systematically in his theological masterpiece *The Ladder of Divine Ascent.*

Saint John of *The Ladder* describes a Hesychast as "he who, being without body, strives to retain his soul within the bounds of its bodily home. A rare and wonderful feat! A hesychast is he who says: 'I sleep but my heart waketh.'"[21] This is a reference to the passage in The Song of Songs 5:2, "I was asleep but my heart was awake." The goal is *theosis*—which is an experience of being transformed by the presence of god, of pure love; it's a constant exchange with the divine from within the heart. And this is what the Hesychast held as the ultimate state of being: union.

To do this, the Hesychasts in Egypt would use the repetition of the Prayer of the Heart to descend (ascend) into the heart. The heart was understood to be far more than the body's most critically functioning organ. The heart was experienced as "a treasure-house." Saint Isaac of Syria explains the sacred aim of the Hesychast: "Try to enter your inner treasure-house and you will see the treasure-house of heaven. For both the one and the other are the same, and one and the same entrance reveals both. The ladder leading to the kingdom is concealed within you, that is, in your soul."[22]

The divine is experienced in the meditation as light, as a light within the heart that's seen or perceived with the nous. The nous is said to have the faculty of direct knowing, or truth, according to the Hesychasts.[23] And this only comes after clearing or cleansing the heart with the repetition of the Prayer of the Heart, *Kyrie Eleison.*

Saint Symeon, the New Theologian from the 10th century, was among the last of what are referred to as the experiential theologians. He believed that spiritual authority comes from within, not from an apostolic appointment by the church. The emphasis of the Hesychasts and the experiential theologians was on this intimate, inner connection to the divine, from within the heart. That inner work had to take place or there couldn't be an authentic transformation, a transformation that only comes from directly knowing or experiencing the soul.

Similar to the Beatitude from Matthew 8: "Blessed are the pure in heart for they shall see god," Saint Simeon explains, "Inasmuch as the heart is purified, so it receives divine grace, and again inasmuch as it receives grace, so it is purified. When this is completed through grace, a man becomes wholly a god."[24]

Professor McGuckin's apartment was covered with the icons of saints his wife had painted; walking into it at Union while I was a divinity student always felt like entering into another world. I knew these saints were alive to them, that they were a part of their inner world as much as they were here depicted with embroidered robes and gold halos on the walls around them.

I knew that as an Eastern Orthodox priest, Professor McGuckin could further my instruction in the Prayer of the Heart that Penny had initiated for me. What I wanted to know was how to pray like a Hesychast. He laughed when I first asked him. Then, when he realized I was serious, he warned me that this form of prayer is meant for the monastic life where you then don't have to go out and cross a busy intersection or interact with the secular world. He explained that what happens by focusing all of our consciousness into the heart is a process that breaks down its walls, leaves it stripped bare and exposed.

My raised eyebrows let him know how great that sounded to me. I was slowly moving through the Old Testament in a compulsory course for graduation, so Ezekiel 36:26 came flying into my mind: "I will remove from your body the heart of stone and give you a heart of flesh."

He went on then to demonstrate the posture the Hesychasts would assume during the recitation of the Prayer of the Heart; they would curl forward, bending their necks and shoulders into an impressive-looking slouch so that they could gaze directly at their chests. And he explained that the breath was controlled during the prayer in the same way that Kundalini yoga focuses on breath with a mantra. Christ's name was invoked with the inhale, and then the petition for mercy came with the exhale. And all along the intention is to drop further into the heart, to remember that the body can be a medium to access the soul, rather than an obstacle.

I tried that posture for the rest of my time as a divinity student and it made me acutely aware of several things. The template for prayer and meditation here is based on a man's body; specifically, on a breast-less chest. When you curl forward with breasts, especially larger ones, the back and neck of the budding Hesychast will scream bloody murder. And you can't enter the heart in a body of pain. Or, yes, you can. But torment of the body is not compulsory. There's no entrance to the heart that reads, "If you're not miserable, come back later."

So, I updated the Hesychast prayer as any Christian (with breasts) in Byzantium might have in the 4th century and instead just acknowledged the body before entering the heart. Whether I was seated or standing, alone or in a crowded room, I just took an intentional breath and recognized with sincere awe that I could not be here without this body.

And instead of focusing on the breath during the prayer, I paid attention to what I sensed once I felt I was really there, in the heart. I took a second intentional breath to acknowledge that the presence of the soul, the nous, is right here, within me. That it takes all of two breaths to be connected again to what's eternal. That I have direct access to divine love at the grocery store, while someone's yelling at me, as I'm signing divorce papers, as my son cries for hours at three in the morning, as I pay bills on a credit card that's nearly at its limit, as that dread comes over me to do more, to be more, to help more, to see the good in myself and others more frequently.

Then I went into the silence, which is like going underwater, or entering dreams while wide awake. The silence is like flipping over in a kayak while whitewater rafting. Let me explain.

I flipped once when I was rafting the Royal Gorge in Colorado as a daredevil teenager. I was in this yellow banana-like kayak with a red helmet on. I felt confident of the technique I had been taught to right myself if I capsized going over the waterfalls we were attempting to raft. I had practiced the technique on dry land and to the approval of the instructors. What I hadn't anticipated was how deafening the roar of the water is beneath the surface. There's a calming, rushing sound we're all used to above ground. But then there's the underside to that sound; there's what the river sounds like from within it.

I'll never forget how disoriented I was, and I don't know if it was because I wasn't expecting it, or if it was simply because the sound itself was so new. I had never heard the clamoring clash of currents under the surface before. I couldn't move at first. I wasn't sure which end was up. My helmet banged against a series of rocks as I scrambled to find the rip cord on the edge of the skirt that sealed me into my kayak. I let go of my paddle so I could search with both hands. And as soon as I found it, I yanked on it with all my upside-down strength could muster.

Going into the heart, for me, is loud like that; it's like hearing the sound of a river from within it. It isn't a silence that we understand as silence. It's not a silence devoid of sound. This silence is the sound of the presence of love within us; and that can be excruciatingly loud. Disorienting even. It's a new voice, meaning, one we're not familiar with, even though it's the most important we could ever hear. It's also new in the sense that it has been hidden from us. Meaning, it's the last place we're taught to look for the voice of god, right here in our own heart.

While I was experimenting as a modern-day Hesychast at Union, I was also in a theatrical course in exegetics. We were divided into pairs of two to act out for the rest of the class a single line from the Old Testament without using words. My partner was a kind, quiet (which worked well here), older bearded man with a limp. We were given Exodus 3, which is about Moses and the burning bush. I had to be the burning bush. I knew how happy it would make me from that day forward to get to say that I performed as the burning bush. (It still cracks me up.) You should have seen the way I pantomimed the hell out of it; my arms flailed up like flames and my face took on a holier-than-though look when "the angel of god" speaks to Moses as a bush on fire.

Our interpretation of this moment was that everything that happened actually took place in the heart. Meaning, a bush engulfed with flames never actually started speaking to Moses. It wasn't like the sound of a voice coming over the intercom when you order drive-thru fast food.

Moses doesn't hear a voice outside him say from this fiery bush, "*Take off your sandals, for the place where you are standing is holy ground."* This is what he hears from within him when he stops herding his sheep for long enough to recognize this miraculous sight; not the vision of the burning bush, but the spirit that moves him to acknowledge the presence of love that has a message for him. From within his own heart.

The burning bush, then, is symbolic of anything in our lives that disrupts us from the habituated routine, the monotony of our everyday, and allows us to return to the presence of love.

Quiet-bearded-man and I demonstrated this by starting and ending our performance with our hands over our hearts. We tried to convey that nothing we were about to do ever really happened. Literally. What we were acting out was the effort of what it takes to remember that no matter what we are doing, or who we are with, or where we are in the world, a mosque, a temple, a yoga studio, a department store, the ground is made instantly holy the moment we're present enough inside our own bodies to hear the presence of love.

The lesson I never forgot, maybe because I acted it out with my body, or maybe because of all the humility it required, and all the humor, was that angels don't speak outside of us. The most sacred voice we can ever hear doesn't have a voice at all. An angel, the voice of god, the presence of love, the voice of the soul, this is the sound of silence. And this truth has been hidden from us, that we contain this chorus. Every one of us.

What has been hidden from us has been hidden within us. What Mary reveals to the other disciples that had been hidden from them is this direct connection to the spiritual world we all contain.

Quiet-Bearded-Man didn't think it was as significant as I did, so we left it out. But I thought it was cool that Moses introduces himself to the bush. (I'm laughing.) After the bush gets his attention, and he lifts his head from herding sheep, he says, "I am Moses." So, in response to this incendiary voice that was actually sounding from inside him, Moses knows who he is. He says his own name.

I thought this was significant because this is what has stayed with me all these years. That this voice of love within us is the truth of who we are. This is how we can move in the world; we can identify with this miraculous, unexpected, uncontrollable, mysterious, and angelic voice of love within us. We can identify with the burning bush. Engulfed by flames but never consumed by them. And in this way, we can live out what has been hidden from us.

How to Meditate Like Mary Magdalene

She said, "I saw the Lord in a vision and I said to him, 'Lord, I saw you today in a vision.' He answered me, 'How wonderful you are for not wavering at seeing me! For where the mind is, there is the treasure.'"

— MARY 7:1–4

Dr. Hal Taussig introduced me more formally to the Gospel of Mary as a professor of biblical literature and early Christianity at Union. He taught a course titled "Loosening Canon" that I took at the same time as McGuckin's course about Hesychasts. Taussig's course let me fall deeper in love with Mary's gospel alongside the texts that help contextualize the discourse that takes place within it; the Gospels of Thomas and Philip in particular.

Years later, at a Barnes & Noble, I stopped suddenly, shocked to see his name in gold lettering across a book titled, *A New, New Testament: A Bible for the 21st Century.* I grabbed it like a psycho and began riffling through the contents. IT BLEW MY MIND. I morphed into a geek theologian right there in the aisle. My mouth was open and everything.

It combines the scripture that was originally included in the formation of the New Testament with the scripture that was excluded, like the Gospel of Mary Magdalene, the Gospel of Thomas, *The Thunder, Perfect Mind,* and *The Acts of Paul and Thecla.*

In the introduction, Taussig explains that with the traditional New Testament, "to know what is inside it, you must know what is outside it." And he gives an example of Paul and Thecla: that you cannot understand Paul (whose conversion story was included in the traditional bible) without also knowing Thecla (whose conversion story was excluded). He describes a fresco dated from approximately 500 A.D. that's painted on the walls of a cave in Turkey. It's of Paul and Thecla, and it depicts them teaching together side by side.

Thecla, as you know, is the fiery Turkish teenager who baptizes herself in the name of Christ, wears men's clothing, and defies patriarchal structures of the 1st century that insisted she marry and have children. Taussig explains that what's included in the New Testament about Paul is incomplete without knowing his relationship to Thecla.

Scholars agree, based not externally on political correctness but internally on linguistic differences, that three of the letters attributed to Paul, 1–2 Timothy and Titus, were written well over a half century after Paul's death. They were created in his name but were in fact reactions to his original views on radical equality for everyone in the Christian community—whether they were Jews or Gentiles, females or males, slaves or free born—which is clearly expressed in Galatians 3:27–28: "For all of you who were baptized into union with Christ clothed yourselves with Christ. There is neither Judean nor Greek, slave nor free, male and female; for in Christ Jesus you are all one."

How then did we arrive at the blatant patriarchal dominance of 1 Timothy 2:11–12? "A woman must learn, listening in silence with all deference. I do not consent to them becoming teachers, or exercising authority over men; they ought not speak." By the 4th century, when the New Testament was being compiled, the radical equality of Christianity was tamed as sexist norms were instituted within the church hierarchy. To really understand 1 Timothy 2:11–12, Taussig suggests you have to look both inside and outside the traditional New Testament. You can't really see what was included and why without also seeing what was excluded.[25]

Taussig organized a committee to very carefully scrutinize which sacred texts should be included in *A New, New Testament*. Men and women, ordained and secular, scholars and monastics, were asked to reach a consensus on which early Christian scripture should represent the various strands of Christianity that existed in the first several centuries before the formation of what became the master story, the singular narrative of Christ captured in the four canonical gospels.

It's hard to explain what seeing all these "conflicting" early Christian texts bound together in one bible did to me. It let me accept the kind of Christian I have always been. Everything else had felt like a compromise, an omission. This wholeness of binding together what "he" said and what "she" said, of what has been seen and unseen, accepted and outcast, including it all, and calling it all Christianity, this to me is what made it sacred, this is what made it scripture.

There's the external and the internal experience of Christ. The metaphysics of what happens when we pray or meditate, this is what Mary's gospel reveals to us. This is what we have been missing. The validation of what we can only meet with and find from within the heart.

Without Mary's gospel, we miss out on the ancient dialogue she had with Christ about this precise practice. Where do we go when we "go within"? What's there waiting for us?

Christ says in the Gospel of Thomas that the kingdom is already spread out upon the earth, if we only have the spiritual capacity to see it. There's a vision we have to acquire, or return to, that allows us to perceive what's here. This is the nous.

Jesuit priest Jean-Yves Leloup describes the nous as a dimension that's often forgotten. In the ancient world, the nous was seen as "the finest point of the soul," or as some might say today, "the angel of the soul."[26] This is the dimension that Mary's gospel alone directly addresses. When Christ says, "For where the mind is, there is the treasure," the word for mind is *nous*. And this is the treasure because this is our direct link to an experience of love, of god, or of the Good, right here in this body. And that return to love is what frees us from the seven powers that bind us to the ego's reality.

The concept of mind in Greek includes the heart; it was never separated from it. This is pre-Descartes, this is before there was an idea that such a division could occur in the body. That we could be a mind devoid of heart. Episcopal priest Cynthia Bourgeault in her masterpiece, *The Meaning of Mary Magdalene*, explains that the nous is a property of the heart, not the mind as we understand *mind* in the Western world. The heart according to the Near Eastern wisdom traditions is an organ of spiritual perception.[27] Merging with the nous, becoming conscious of it within the heart, and seeing with its vision, this is the goal of the process of inner transformation that the Gospel of Mary relates Christ underwent and that we can all undergo as well.

Bourgeault believes that the Gospel of Mary could potentially be proof that Mary Magdalene was a witness not only to Christ's resurrection but to the entire transformation he went through. If she had merged with the nous, if she could see with the spiritual eye of the heart, which is a vision that allows us to see through death, to be a love that exists beyond it, then she never left him, not physically or psychically. She witnessed the way he freed himself from the bonds of death, how he remembered the nous, and created a spiritual blueprint for us all to follow.

The Gospel of Mary Magdalene, then, according to Bourgeault, has preserved in visionary form through the pure, unflinching nous of Mary Magdalene, the moment "when universal salvation gushed forth from Jesus's cosmological act of atonement."[28]

I think this is how we pray, how we meditate, like Mary Magdalene. We return to love within us, within the heart, quietly, discreetly, and we don't ask for any reward or external affirmation in exchange for doing the work. The return to love is the treasure itself.

This is why she was so wonderful, according to Christ. He calls her wonderful, I think, because of the unique bravery it takes to return to the love within you. She returned to the nous, which is the aspect of the soul that we can be conscious of while living, while here in this human body.

And I don't think union was a constant state for her. I think it's something she became adept at remembering. Union is hard won. Merging with the nous, the angel of the soul, becoming one, this is as gritty as it gets when it comes to spiritual work.

I think it's a state we can all work at cultivating. It happens where no one else can see or validate for us that we're doing the work. It's feminine, it's internal. It's direct experience. It happens quietly, within, when instead of reacting from the ego, we take a moment and respond differently.

For example, as I moved through the years, out of Union, into and out of a marriage, raising a son, I found that the desire to love was enough. A desire to see with this spiritual eye of the heart was enough to allow for these tiny transformations all throughout the day. I couldn't curl forward over my heart all day like the Hesychasts, so I just took three intentional breaths whenever I felt one of those seven powers of the ego arise. A breath to descend into the heart, a second breath to connect to the soul, the nous, and then a third breath, to surface and know I'm being led by love.

I called this the soul-voice meditation, and eventually, I would hang out in my heart for hours on end. Just listening. Asking questions and receiving answers.

My beloved, crazy, navel-gazing Hesychasts experienced the nous as containing a faculty of direct knowing, or unmediated truth.[29] This isn't something we need outside sources to confirm, or people we love and trust to validate for us. This is something that's in the bones. Or that's how it feels to me. It feels like blood memory. Like something I couldn't possibly learn, from anyone or anywhere. It's the other side of education. It's what we can only become aware of from within.

The Trappist monk and author Thomas Merton describes the nous as "a pure diamond, blazing with the invisible light of heaven." The invisible light of heaven. This is what I think Christ means when he says in the Gospel of Thomas that the kingdom is already here, spread out all over the earth, if we only had the eyes to see it.

The Red Egg

Have you already found the beginning, then, that you seek for the end? For where the beginning is the end will be. Blessed is the one who stands at the beginning: that one will know the end and will not taste death.

— The Gospel of Thomas

I shot up in bed with one of those gasps, a sharp intake of air, like I'd been held underwater for too long. It felt like three in the morning. Everything was silent in that interstice type way, suspended between night and day. I can't even imagine how hysterical my face must have looked. Shock had my eyebrows clear up to my hairline. My face was buckling under the strain of trying to comprehend what I was feeling. I probably looked like an astronaut undergoing high G-force centrifuge training.

I sat there in the dark wide-awake, beside my sleeping fiancé, trying to figure out what I had felt and why I was terrified by it. It was the holiest moment I had ever experienced.

I knew several things all at once. I was pregnant, I was having a boy, and he would be solid, big-boned. He would be a real concrete presence.

He felt like something that just a second before had been ephemeral and otherworldly and was now a fixed being tethered to me for all of eternity.

And I use the word eternity intentionally here because I felt like I knew it. I understood it. And this is what scared the hell out of me. I think the idea of it has always comforted me. *Ah, how nice, we live on forever.* But the actual breath of it, the glimpse I felt during my son's conception, just utterly freaked me out. We never end. And this is what I was repeating as I started crying, trying to digest, and comprehend, everything I knew then.

We don't have an ending.

What I knew about eternity didn't come from my mind. My body was telling me. We never end. And I sat there, like that, crying because I was so terrified and so insanely happy.

I had never heard of conscious conception, that it was a thing, like conversion stories, or near-death experiences. I didn't know this genre existed. That other women also were aware of the moment when they conceived. I sat there feeling alone and like a freak, which is like home base for every woman I've ever known. *New experience = I'm a freak.* It's the go-to conclusion.

This was also before the expression "zero fucks given" came into common usage. But this is what began to descend on me. I began to give absolutely zero fucks about how I would ever explain this to anyone. I felt this righteous need to just validate it myself. THIS HAPPENED. And this scared the shit out of me and this was the holiest moment I've ever known. Yes, utter paradox. And yes, no apologies.

It made me think of how our concept of god would be so different if all along, from the time of the Venus von Willendorf period of prehistory, roughly 30,000 B.C.E., to right now, we'd never swung around and done a 180 from worshipping the goddess to just worshipping a god. Think of the sermons! The rituals! The ceremonies! Think of how much they would change if we were equally hearing from both sexes about what it's like to find god in the body.

The liturgy and the laws would shift dramatically, I think. Because for me, the experience was like the universe huffed on me. I felt like for one instant, or maybe an eternity, I really got how massively beyond my comprehension this being human is. That's it. I was humbled senseless.

I have zero clue about anything ultimate, or how it works, or why I got to be the mother of this particular son. This one that I recognized the second I saw him. As if his face had always been missed, as if I always knew the shape of it. As if he existed in me all along.

Layne Redmond, in *When the Women Were Drummers,* explains, "All the eggs a woman will ever carry form in her ovaries when she's a four-month-old fetus in the womb of her mother. This means our cellular life as an egg begins in the womb of our grandmother. Each of us spent five months in our grandmother's womb."

In Robert Lentz's icon, Mary Magdalene is pointing with one hand at an egg held in her other hand. She's staring straight at the viewer with a gaze to me that translates as something like "Everything comes from within." And there's an insistence, or maybe an exasperation, almost "How can you not see this?"

It struck me the first time I saw her icon, that the egg is the most feminine object or symbol of creation. In modern cosmology, it is believed that 13 billion years ago the entire mass of the universe was compressed into a gravitational singularity, the so-called cosmic egg. And from that singularity, the universe has expanded ever since to its current state, and continues at the moment you're reading this to expand further still.

The look on Mary's face in Lentz's iconography suggests she understood a secret we're still trying to work out. She's trying to point us to it, literally. To help us realize and remember it. That all life comes from within. Or as Jung realizes, in *The Red Book,* "I am the egg that surrounds and nurtures the seed of the God in me."

I've had this icon of Mary Magdalene pointing at an egg with me for almost two decades now. It's the first object I find a nook for every time I move. It's the same icon Dr. Karen King put on the cover of her translation of Mary's gospel.

According to the Eastern Orthodox Church, Mary Magdalene is associated with Easter because Christ resurrected to her first. I'll return to this again later, this Easter moment and why love is what brings us back to life. But after hearing this in seminary about Mary, that she really is the whole reason Easter happens, I found it so curious that we associate an Easter egg with a rabbit rather than Mary.

The Germanic tradition of the Easter Bunny dates back only to the 18th century with German Anglican immigrants and a myth about an *Osterhase* who gave gifts of candy and colored eggs to good children, sort of like a tiny, hairy Santa Claus. The Orthodox Church used to have a tradition of fasting from eggs during Lent, so the colored hard-boiled eggs were used as a way to celebrate breaking the fast on Easter morning.

There's a more ancient legend, though, that associates the egg with Easter. The Eastern Orthodox tradition holds that after the resurrection, Mary Magdalene traveled to Rome, where she was admitted to the court of Tiberius Caesar because of her high social standing. She told the court the story of her love for Christ, and how poorly justice was served under Pontius Pilate during Christ's trial. She told Caesar that Christ had risen. And to help explain his resurrection, supposedly, she took an egg from off of the feast laid out before them.

If I could magically pick to be present at any moment in history, this would be it. I would be sitting there held rapt with attention to every word Mary gave during her first sermon. I've imagined what she might have said so many times. I've imagined how it would correct for us this ancient misunderstanding we have about the body, and about the soul.

It varies because sometimes there's this loud thread of exasperation. As if she has been pointing at the egg after all these years, after millennia, and we still have zero clue.

But it goes something like this . . .

An egg, like a seed, contains the end at the beginning. The seed already has the bloom held within it. The egg holds safely inside whatever new life its precariously fragile shell is meant to protect. And if that new life is going to emerge, it has to come from within. You can't break a shell and still expect a little beak to one day peck its way out and into the world. You have to let that tiny creature with wings within the shell arrive at the day of its own birth. You have to remain in this trusting, quiet unknown, as every mother or artist knows, and let that life declare its existence not when your ego says it's time, but when that new life is ready.

A body, like an egg, contains a soul.

In the beginning there's the dark, there's the womb, and the only light is the soul, this new life that waits to emerge from within. The soul is the beginning, and also the end. Birth is meant to happen before we die. Ideally, many times. But we have to die to the ego to let it. The more the soul rises, resurrects in this life, the more love is present here inside us. Meaning, the soul is all we are when we come into this life and it's all that we'll be when we leave it. If you can stand there at the beginning, then you'll know the end, which is a love that only ever expands.

Then according to legend, Caesar was like, "Hah, yeah, right. A person can no more resurrect than that egg in your hand turn red."

(The egg immediately turns red.)

The Body Never Lies

What you say, you say in a body; you can say nothing outside this body.
You must awaken while in this body, for everything exists in it:
Resurrect in this life.

— The Gospel of Philip

There came a point when words were no longer useful. I sank into this clear-cut knowing of what needed to be done. Every move I made was intentional, unequivocal. And that certainty, that blazing truth spoke for itself. I began to experience how much less I can do, for the rest of my life, if I choose. The body never lies. Letting go of the need to explain myself with words, of saying why I needed to do something, or when, was the most powerful I have ever been.

So, for example, when the midwives wheeled over a huge-ass floor-length mirror, the kind you'd check your outfit in before going out, and started positioning it so I could see my son's head emerging, all I needed to do was allow it to not exist. I didn't need to get angry, to tell them to get that thing out of my face, or my fanny, rather. I just continued doing what I had been doing, which was everything I already knew I needed to do in order to get my son safely into the world. My inside was my outside. I was nothing more or less than who I am.

I didn't need to explain to them that seeing his image outside of me was a distraction. It took me away from the awareness I already had from within. The image the mirror provided was awareness once removed. I already had direct awareness. I could see him but with a sense the heart's capable of, a far broader and more precise sight than the eyes will ever provide for us.

I could sense that something was wrong, that his position was making it difficult for him to descend. I knew in a way I couldn't translate that he was healthy and strong and that he would make it through this, that I would birth him and not need the C-section they had alerted the surgeon I was headed toward. I never said a word, though. I never said anything except the passionate repetition of one name, and this is the part of my birth story it has taken years (and this book) to reconcile. Because the body never lies.

Forty-eight hours earlier, I'd been warned that I was going to need to be induced the next morning. So, my husband and I walked the full length of Manhattan. We ate an amazing meal, had some red wine, and some impressive sex. (Impressive because of my size.) Then that night, I stood up from the couch in my little black maternity dress and my water broke. It wasn't biblical, but it felt like a triumph. I started to strut around the apartment, "They can't induce me now!" With the tiny flood, came breath-clenching contractions. When I arrived at the hospital, I was already at three and a half centimeters dilated. I come from a long line of natural-child-birthing women. I siphoned my confidence from this fact. And trusted I would be counted among them.

I went into the hospital shower and stood with my hands braced against the wall to support me as each new and more painful contraction wracked my body. The hot water pounded against the center of my back and slid over my sacrum, soothing me when the painful contractions receded. I use the word *pain,* but this isn't accurate. At all. Pain doesn't begin to describe what would happen in intervals to my entire being. Here, I have it now. It felt as if slowly, and with greater success, I was being de-boned. It felt as if my pelvis was being pushed in increments down through my body from the pressure of each contraction. I labored that way for most of the night.

Before dawn, I moved back to the bed for the midwife to check on me. I knew from the look on her face as her gloved hand gently investigated that she wasn't finding what she had hoped. I could read her as if her thoughts were written on cue cards out in front of her. It was not good news. She said that I had actually gone down a centimeter. I was now only at two and a half centimeters dilated. Up until this point, I had been managing the "de-boning" with breath work, and the hot water, and sheer, undiluted resolve. And it all felt worth it, because it was productive. But exhaustion and dread began to set in after I realized I had labored for all that time and had actually managed to close myself back up again. I had managed to labor in the wrong direction.

As I remember it now, I went straight into the unimaginable pain. It was worse than being de-boned. It felt as if all along, without me realizing it or any doctor seeing it on an X-ray or sonogram machine, my pelvis was actually made of a thick, translucent glass. And my son's small but hard bowling ball of a head had gotten itself wedged into this miraculous glass-pelvis in a way where instead of managing through it, of finding a way to shift and turn so that he could fit, his skull had actually shattered it. My pelvis shattered into infinitesimal shards of glass and with each next contraction the countless shards pierced me from the inside out.

I can't really say that I said his name. The first time I heard myself say it, I didn't even realize it was me calling out for him. This was the point where words no longer served a purpose. This was the point where I crossed a threshold I knew I could never come back from.

With each next wave of the shards of glass embedding themselves deeper into my body, I now only said his name, again and again. Jesus Christ. And I didn't know until pain had embodied me so fully that this existed; that he was a truth that lived within me beyond words and reason. The only truth real enough to match the intensity of that pain. As if the pain was a flamethrower, and with each next contraction, it consumed everything within me that wasn't real, until all that remained was this stowaway love that had always been there. A love that I had fought against, a love that I had denied, a love that I built an iron wall around my heart to keep me safe from, a love I never needed to find, a love that has been with me my entire life from the inside out.

I never needed to ask for an epidural. It was communicated so clearly through the state I had entered. I remember the nod I gave my husband. It was a nod so telling, he just immediately set out to find the doctor. She was a vision as she entered the room. She was at least six months pregnant, maybe seven. This felt like a blessing. Her headscarf was as white as her white medical coat.

I was still calling his name as if it was the only panacea or elixir for managing the pain. So, she followed suit, and began repeating, "Allah" with each next contraction until I could hold still for long enough for her to insert that horrifically long needle into my spine. We locked eyes as the medication began to reach my shattered glass-pelvis and coat it with numbness, which felt like warm honey. We locked eyes and said nothing, and said everything we could ever need to communicate. Because everything in that moment was human, and everything was holy.

Mary Magdalene Was Not a Prostitute

I said to him, "So, now, Lord, does a person who sees a vision see it with the soul or with the spirit?" The Savior answered, "A person does not see with the soul or with the spirit. Rather the mind, which exists between these two, sees the vision and that is what . . ."

— MARY 7:5–7

I remember how WTF I felt when I first saw that this passage from chapter seven in Mary's gospel gets cut off right at the clincher. All three copies of Mary's gospel have this same answer torn from it. We can only imagine what Christ was about to tell Mary.

The gospel won't start up again until four pages later. And it also resumes mid-sentence, as if we passed out just before Christ was going to tell us how we perceive a vision from within, and then we wake up again while Mary's telling us about the powers that keep the soul bound.

There is so much we don't know. There's so much I don't know. I've been studying Mary Magdalene for two decades as a scholar, as a theologian, and as a devout seeker compelled by a force I can't name or entirely understand to know who she really was, and to interpret the significance of her gospel.

And the effort has humbled me.

There is so much that just remains a mystery. This is why I love humility. Whenever I let it sweep over me, it's like changing into flats after realizing I had been in high heels for too long.

There's so much that we don't have empirical truth to rest on when speaking about her and who she was. There is, however, one thing we know for certain: Mary Magdalene was not a prostitute.

And this is not a commentary about prostitution. I often get a wave of defense when I've written or spoken about this before. But this is not about sex workers, and the sacredness of the body. Though I appreciate that Mary Magdalene has been the patroness of those who have felt shamed by our culture in relation to the body for centuries. And I think there's beauty in the story, that she was a prostitute. There's beauty in a story of a woman who loved much and was forgiven much. It's a story of the sinner turned saint. And who can't identify with that? It's a good story. It's just not Mary Magdalene's story. And it's simply not true.

Meaning, there's so much we can't verify. So much of the evidence, the scripture that would attest to the truth of who she was, has been tampered with, burned, edited, or destroyed. (The most damaging of which is the capacity of our imagination to even conceive of the idea that she may have been the most significant figure in Christ's life. Because of two millennia of homilies and sermons, and interpretations of her as a prostitute rather than as one of the first apostles in the earliest form of the church.) But her status as a prostitute *is* verifiable. And it's not true.

So, what happened?

How did Mary Magdalene become the penitent prostitute?

If Christian theologians in the Latin West were going to establish an exclusively male church, then the central figure to Christ's story, Mary Magdalene, needed to be retold.

Starting in the 4th century, with the formation of the traditional bible, all of the gospels that confirmed Mary's spiritual authority and unique relationship with Christ were excluded from the canon and deemed "heretical," like the Gospel of Mary Magdalene, the Gospel of Philip, and the Gospel of Thomas. And the scriptures that confirmed and validated women's leadership in the earliest forms of Christianity, like *The Acts of Paul and Thecla,* were also excluded.

Over the centuries, Christ became less and less human; he was depicted as chaste, monastic, purely divine, and Mary Magdalene underwent the inverse transformation. She became more and more human, more "sinful," until the 6th century when Pope Gregory sealed the deal on her depiction in his interpretation of Christ healing Mary by freeing her of seven "demons."

Pope Gregory conflated Mary Magdalene as both the unnamed "sinner" in Luke 7 who anointed Christ's feet, and the Mary of Luke 8 and Mark 16 who is freed of all her demons by Christ. And then he interpreted these passages as confirming that Mary's sinfulness had to do with her sexuality. "Seven demons" translated to him as prostitute, no question.

Or as Cynthia Bourgeault explains, "The shadow side of Christianity's notoriously undealt-with issues around human sexuality and the feminine get projected directly onto her."[30]

Pope Gregory's Homily 33 set the precedent that the faithful should hold Mary as the penitent whore.[31] This interpretation of Mary had a very clear agenda: reinforce the view that women were to be seen primarily in terms of their sexuality and not their spiritual nature. Dr. Karen King explains that his fiction of Mary Magdalene as the whore created by the church solved two problems at once; it undermined both "the teachings associated with Mary and women's capacity to take on leadership roles."[32] With this interpretation of Mary, as the penitent prostitute, as King laments, "Her radical heritage had been tamed and erased."[33]

Finally, in 1969, which, if we do the math, is 1,378 years after Gregory's fusion of Mary Magdalene and the unnamed sinner as proof of her prostitution, the church officially corrected his mistake, or, to be clear, his misogyny. (And this admission came 450 years after religious scholars had rejected it as fiction, as just flat-out historically inaccurate.) However, the image and interpretation of Mary Magdalene as the penitent prostitute continues to be preached; it has remained in place behind the pulpit and deep-set in the popular imagination.

July 22 is Mary Magdalene's feast day in the Catholic tradition. (I'm writing this chapter on July 22, 2018.) She was recently "rehabilitated" from the penitent prostitute to the apostle to the apostles by Pope Francis. (I knew good things would come from a Pope who knows how to tango.) Though, it's important to make clear, she is still not considered an apostle herself. (Let alone the first.)

So, we've established what religious historians, and now even the Pope, know she was not.

Mary Magdalene was not a prostitute.

What, then, do we know about her that isn't fiction?

Let's start with this. The historical figure Mary of Magdala was a prominent Jewish woman, a benefactress of Jesus's ministry, a visionary, and a leading apostle in the earliest Christian movement. Her status as the apostle to the apostles comes from this "secret" teaching, or transmission, that she receives from Christ, according to her gospel.

Her epithet "Magdalene" comes from the fact that she was born in the town of Magdala (located in present-day Israel), on the west shore of the Sea of Galilee just north of the city of Tiberias. And although Mary Magdalene is often depicted as having red hair and culver white skin (as if from Ireland), it's more historically accurate to depict her as if from ancient Israel.

According to the canonical gospels, Mary Magdalene was present at the crucifixion, she was there at the burial, and she was there alone at the empty tomb. And she is the first to witness the resurrection. Let me say that again: Mary Magdalene was the one Christ resurrected to. In the Gospel of John, Christ gives Mary Magdalene special instructions and commissions her to be the one to announce the good news. Her. She is the one he chooses.

The word *apostle* comes from the Greek *apostolos*, meaning "one who is sent." Mary's status as the apostle to the apostles also comes from this moment when Mary is the one who is sent by Christ to tell the other disciples that he has resurrected. Without her capacity to receive this vision of Christ from within her, to see that he had risen, the other disciples would not have become apostles themselves.

Mary Magdalene is one of the main speakers in several 1st- and 2nd-century texts recording dialogues of Christ with his disciples after the resurrection, like *The Sophia of Jesus Christ*, from the

2nd century, where Mary is one of the seven women (and twelve men) who gathered to hear Christ after the resurrection.[34] Also the 3rd-century text, the *Pistis Sophia*, where Mary is preeminent among the disciples, because, as Christ explains in it, "You are she whose heart is more directed to the Kingdom of Heaven than all your brothers."[35]

And in the Gospel of Philip, whose Coptic version dates to 250 A.D. and whose Greek version dates even farther back, to 150 A.D., Mary is named as the companion of Christ. The word in Greek is *koinonos*. It translates as companion, partner, or consort. Logion 55 of the Gospel of Philip, reads, "The companion [*koinonos*] of the Son is Miriam of Magdala. The Teacher loved her more than all the disciples; he often kissed her on the mouth."[36]

The Gospel of Mary Magdalene confirms that Mary had gone through a process that allowed her to "see" Christ from within her. She could receive a vision of him. And the fact that Mary can see Christ, according to her gospel, is the proof that she has become "a child of true humanity," the *anthropos*, fully human, and fully divine. That process involved going through the seven powers of the ego, which is how I interpret the seven "demons," in order to unbind her soul—or in order to remember that she is also a soul, and not just this mortal, stressed-out, perpetually threatened ego that will die with the body in death.

Before Christ gets cut off by whoever found his full response to Mary's question too incendiary for us to know, he tells her that a person sees a vision with the "mind," which is between the soul and the spirit. And we know at this point that the Greek word for mind, *nous*, is actually the highest aspect of the soul, "the soul's angel," the aspect of the soul we can perceive while embodied. This is what the Hesychast experienced as existing within the heart, that treasure house inside us. The nous is like the microphone, or the movie projector, within the heart that translates the ancient and amazing truths our own soul wants to say to us, while we're here, living, and can still use this tremendous opportunity of being an embodied soul, to evolve.

Rumi suggests that "everyone sees the unseen in proportion to the clarity of their hearts." This is what I think Mary Magdalene achieved through this process her gospel relates. I think Mary had clarity of heart, and this is how and why she could perceive Christ.

So why now, after nearly two millennia of being misunderstood, her spiritual authority, her ministry, and her gospel being buried and silenced, why is she now rising in stature? Why are we suddenly curious (and even reverent) about this woman who has stood in plain daylight as the central figure in Christ's life?

If you asked me this, first I would tell you that truth is a phoenix and can never be burned; truth will always emerge from the ashes and find its way to the surface of our consciousness.

Next, I would tell you that I think we are finally ready for her teachings, for the other half of the story that began not with Christ's birth but with his resurrection. The story of a potential we all possess while we're human to be the bridge between heaven and earth. The story of a woman who was beloved to Christ not because she followed him, or worshipped him like an idol or a being far greater than she could ever be. But rather, because she followed his example and became the love that he was also.

And I would tell you that this love she became is what our world needs most desperately. It's a love that renders all things sacred, from the animals to the angels, from the poorest to the most powerful. It's a love that sees the inherent worth in all living things. Mary Magdalene is the embodiment of a love that reaches where it never has before.

Mary Magdalene is most associated with Easter, with the resurrection, because she was the one there at the tomb, the one who waited in the dark, past his death and absence. She was the one he resurrected to. She was the first to see him, and she only recognized it was him when he called her by name.

But let's back up.

I think it's significant to realize that she didn't just happen to be there, in the right place at the right time. There's a prominence inherent in the fact that she was the one to be there, to see him first. There's a love we've overlooked for so long. The human love between two people, as a love that never ends. And I think it's time we recognize it.

I have always wondered how the story of the resurrection would shift fundamentally if we realized it was also a story about a love we all possess. That when we can let love reach where it has never been before, out past the ego's idea of the self, then we quite literally come back to life. We die, and resurrect. Hopefully several times at least before we pass away, into whatever's next for us.

In Chapter 20 of the Gospel of John, titled "The Risen Life," from *A New, New Testament,* Mary is weeping from the loss of Christ's body outside the empty tomb and then she sees two angels clothed in white, standing there where the body of Christ had been. I've always loved this for two reasons. First, that she can see angels at all. But second, and more significantly, that when she's at her most human, sobbing, and feeling separate from Christ, when she's at her most broken, and vulnerable, this is when she can perceive the angels.

And they ask her, "Why are you weeping?" They ask from their position of already knowing that she can never be separate from Christ, that he is in fact already standing right behind her. She lets them know that she's crying because she misses his physical form. She loved him entirely, body and soul. And then she turns, and Christ asks her the exact same question the angels asked her, "Why are you weeping?" But she doesn't know yet this presence she sees before her; she thinks he's the gardener. And so, she repeats her need to tend to his actual flesh, to find his human form and care after it. This is when he calls out to her, "Mary." And in hearing her name in his voice, she knows again that Christ is with her, that he had in fact never left.

I've always imagined that although physically she was at the tomb, in the garden of a cemetery, she met with Christ in a place that's far less literal, and far more difficult to describe. I've imagined that this meeting she has with him takes place not because of sight but because of vision. I think she could perceive him with a spiritual aperture that exists only in the heart.

It's a re-education to see Mary Magdalene as an apostle, as a beloved disciple Christ considered worthy enough to want to return to first. Worthy enough to want to have her as his witness. To come to her, in the dark, beyond death, because he knew she was the one who could see him with her heart.

It's a re-education to think that Christ needed Mary's love in order to resurrect, in order to be witnessed. Just as the angels need us to know how worthy we are to perceive them.

I love imagining that his ministry and hers are still inextricably linked. That his purpose was fulfilled because she was there to meet him. That he was only able to bridge heaven and earth because of the human love between them. I love to imagine that we might still have a love story to unearth. A love that has been age after age, making its way to the surface of our consciousness. A love that we are finally ready for.

A love that is as human as it is divine.

No One Was There to Witness the Witness

And Desire said, "I did not see you go down, yet now I see you go up. So why do you lie since you belong to me?" The soul answered, "I saw you. You did not see me nor did you know me. You mistook the garment I wore for my true self. And you did not recognize me."

— Mary 9:2–6

I want to return to the resurrection, again. It is so much more significant than we have ever given it credit for—that Mary and Christ were together first when he resurrected. That he came back to her, for her. Or this is how I see it.

Mary Magdalene exclaims in Hebrew, "*Rabboni!*"—or Teacher—according to John 20:16. After he calls out to her, after she recognizes him by hearing her name in his voice. This is an intimate exchange. She is his witness, not by accident. She is there because she is a part of the story of how and why he was able to rise.

And then Christ says the line that has confused so many for so long: *Noli me tangere,* Latin for, as many have translated it, do not touch me. A more apt translation is, do not cling to me. And this is what makes sense in the trajectory of his ministry.

He was all about sitting with outcasts, eating with untouchables, and drinking from the well with the Samaritan woman. It just makes zero sense that suddenly, once no longer incarnate, he would get squeamish over a woman's touch, a woman he loved the most.

This has been misinterpreted to emphasize Christ's purity and chastity (and also women's power to defile the holy). And it has been held up as further proof of Mary's "sinful" status as the penitent prostitute. The idea is that Christ is telling her, essentially, don't touch me because I haven't ascended to god yet, meaning, you might mess with my ascension.

Artistic depictions of this moment, for example Italian Renaissance artist Correggio's *Noli Me Tangere,* place Christ above Mary, who is usually below him on her knees or at his feet. Christ's one hand is pointed up, indicating his ascension, and his other hand is, well, giving Mary the hand. He's depicted as blocking her from coming near him.

But there's a different translation of this moment that has to do with the spiritual path he had mastered and that he had led Mary Magdalene through, to completion. The kenotic path, a spiritual path of self-emptying love. The core practice of this path is to not cling to anything. Not even to her own beloved, Christ. It's to disengage "the egoic operating system" and "upgrade" consciousness by descending into the heart.

In Christian theology, *kenosis* is the Greek word for the act of emptying. It's the act of releasing the ego's idea, or will, and allowing the divine will to act through us. But how do we do this?

When we are gripped by something or someone the ego desires, how do we practice this path?

We are missing so much of Christ's response to Mary's question of how a person perceives a vision, through what aperture, with what spiritual faculty. We are missing four pages of his answer and also presumably his instruction in how we then practice or use this spiritual capacity to perceive with the nous, within the heart. Mary could be speaking about what stages Christ led her soul through, and here we are at the third, desire, when the gospel starts back up again in Mary 9:2.

Egoic desire, or craving, thinks that the soul "belongs" to it. And because of this, the ego cannot recognize the soul. It has always haunted me when the soul says, "I saw you. You did not see me." The soul can see the ego. But the ego can't recognize the soul: "You mistook the garment I wore for my true self. And you did not recognize me." The soul is saying here to the ego's desire, I am not this body, not essentially. I am what exists before the body and after. But if you are only focusing on the body, on the egoic garment I am wearing as a soul, you will not recognize me.

What this means to me happens, actually, every day. It's very ordinary. It's referring to those moments when we get so caught up in what we want, we can't see the bigger picture. We cling to the outcome like a lemur. And, if you're like me, we obsess about it. We go around and around blind as a bat, missing out on the present moment because we're so clenched to this idea of what we think we want.

And what Mary's gospel is saying in this passage is that the key is to become unattached, to try not to touch and cling. To release our little lemur hands from around the desired "object" and trust that a will greater than our ego has things covered for us in ways we can hardly imagine.

There will be seven "demons," or powers that test the soul and try to bind the soul to the ego. The way the soul moves through this power of desire, and all of the climates of the ego, is simply to let go of all attachments, all judgments we might have. This immediately frees the soul. (For that moment.)

I've always been a little suspicious of what Christ said to Mary in John 20:17. Because after all, Mary not only was the first to witness the resurrection, but was also the only one there. No one was there to witness the witness. No one actually heard Christ say to Mary, "*Noli me tangere*."

I love the translation of this moment in *A New, New Testament*. Christ says to Mary, "Do not hold on to me." (The idea that this is in response to Mary trying to touch Christ or reach for him is actually an interpretation; it's not stated within scripture that she did.) "Do not hold on to me" feels like a comment to reinforce this path of self-emptying love.

Noli me tangere is Christ's reminder to Mary that there's no need to reach for his physical form. He's not outside her, appearing before her in the gardens by the empty tomb. He's still where he has always been, and will never leave. Inside the walls of her mystical heart.

Noli me tangere, beloved. There is no need to touch me, to cling to me, to hold on to my physical form. I am with you, from within you.

The Power to Judge

[The soul] came to the third Power, which is called ignorance.
It examined the soul closely, saying, "Where are you going?
You are bound by wickedness . . ." and the soul said,
"Why do you judge me, since I have not passed judgment."

— MARY 9:8–13

In the gospel of Mary, Mary 9:8, ignorance calls the soul "bound by wickedness." (Which always makes me laugh. It's what makes ignorance ignorant. It calls out in others what it can't see in itself.)

Ignorance is the power, or the frame of mind, we all enter into when we have so aligned with the ego that we think we are in a place to judge. And most often if we are judging someone else, we are doing a number on ourselves, also. We're quietly pouring corrosives into our heart with words that judge where we are on this path that leads back to the heart.

Another word for ignorance is unconsciousness. And this is what can be so tricky about ignorance. We are unaware, unconscious of what we are doing when we judge others and ourselves. And the more we do it, the more it clings to us; judge and we are judged.

The canonical gospels emphasize the importance of releasing judgment. In Luke 6:37, "Do not judge, and you will not be judged; do not condemn, and you will not be condemned. Forgive, and you will be forgiven." And, in Matthew 7:1–2, "Do not judge and you will not be judged. For just as you judge others, you will yourselves be judged, and the standard that you use will be used for you."

And in the Gospel of Mary, the soul makes clear that judgment is the only real obstacle that keeps us from a return to consciousness, to love. The soul continues to move through these powers, or to face these inner demons, by refusing to judge. The soul refuses to pass judgment. Because judgment is what binds us then to that power, that demon, that thought or fear.

Why does this matter, and how is this relevant to you?

It matters because we oppress ourselves. Or we continue the work of the oppressor, if we've been terrorized or traumatized into silence. We silence ourselves from within before we even dare to speak. (And there's no judgment for how long each of us needs to stay silent. It has taken me years to write about Mary Magdalene because I constantly judged everything I wrote as not good enough.) This power to judge keeps us in our place. Keeps us small and bottled up. Keeps us contained, restricted to the same pathways that have existed before.

This is what silences us from within us. This power to judge, if it remains unrecognized, is what keeps us from ever really expressing the truth of who we are.

The Red Spring

I have been bound, but I have not bound anything.
They did not recognize me, but I have recognized that the universe
is to be dissolved, both the things of earth and those of heaven.

—Mary 9:14–15

If I could give you an aerial view, like a drone, that starts slightly above our little eco-hut, so you can see how close we are to the Tor (peak) in Glastonbury; it looks as if we're at the base of it. And as the view draws closer to the huge windows that line the living room and look out over the stunningly verdant English countryside, you'd see three people all facing the window in workout gear, barely holding it together as they tried to keep up with a Beyoncé-themed workout blaring from the iPad propped up on a table in front of them. Modern pilgrims at their best.

Christiane let me borrow one of her cashmere sweaters the next morning. It was far colder than I had thought it would be in September. Her book *Goddesses Never Age* and my book *How to Love Yourself (and Sometimes Other People)* had both just come out. So we had flown over to London together for events, and Kyle, my Scottish soul mate, had picked us up and taken us to Glastonbury. It was so picturesque I felt like I was in a photo shoot for *Town and Country*. Little gorgeous white-as-snow sheep dotted the impossibly bright-green hillside.

We started our hike up the Tor, Christiane and I just kind of taking it all in with a stroll, and Kyle bounding up before us with his boundless energy. We could hear him screaming once he had reached the top, even though we still had far to go. We locked eyes and started laughing.

The Tor in Glastonbury is supposedly where the Red and the White Spring originate. Avalon, the sacred isle, or the Isle of the Blest, is thought of as representing the symbolic world center, with the Tor as the *axis mundi*, the world axis, that joins the ordinary world with the regions above and below.

The Red Spring represents the goddess, or the divine feminine, and the White Spring represents the godhead, or the divine masculine. The Red Spring emerges in a well that has been surrounded and protected by a garden since the 1950s. And the White Spring is in the care of the White Spring Trust, a group of devoted residents who tend to it and keep the candles lit around the caldron where the White Spring emerges.

Celtic legends relate a sacred relationship between wells and cauldrons, and the alchemists produce red and white elixirs in alchemy in their attempts to produce the "alchemical wedding" or the coniunctio, the union of opposites. This, the alchemists believed, created the Philosopher's stone, the holy grail, the waters of everlasting life.

The goal of the alchemist was to take base metals and, through a process of purification, transform them into unalloyed gold. This, of course, is a perfect metaphor for taking the base emotions of the ego, like envy and rage, and transforming them into the singular awareness of the soul.

Gold was the metaphor for discovering the true spiritual nobility of the soul while still embodied. The ultimate objective is to restore the bond between matter and spirit, between earth and heaven, between masculine and feminine, between all those "opposites" that create this illusion of separateness. The ultimate objective is union.

Legends relate that Joseph of Arimathea, a relative of Christ, traveled to Glastonbury from Palestine, through Southern France, carrying with him two small cruets and the cup that Christ used at the Last Supper. Supposedly, these two cruets, depicted as red and white, carried the blood and the water that came from Christ's wounds at his crucifixion. Joseph built the first church in Avalon and buried the cup and the two cruets somewhere between the Red Spring and the White Spring.

So, although the springs are separate, Red and White, they rise from the same source, from the axis between the worlds, the Tor. There is a seven-tiered labyrinth that surrounds the Tor, to represent the sevenfold process of transformation. The last phase in alchemy, the rubedo, or reddening, refers to the union of opposites restored, the royal marriage achieved from within the heart. The lunar-goddess-queen and the solar-god-king remembered as one.

We descended from the Tor, and Kyle took us into town to explore. As we walked along a narrow street, Kyle spotted a storefront that said, "Aura Photography" and immediately insisted that we all get one done. Christiane's was so surreal. We marveled at the otherworldly colors, hues of the most luminous periwinkle. Her photo looked like several gorgeous purple angels were sitting on her lap. Kyle's was a full-on rainbow. He gave it one look and nodded his head, "Of course." And my photo just showed layer after layer of the most crimson and scarlet reds I had ever seen.

The aura man felt sorry for me and started explaining the baseness of the color red, how it represents anger and attachments to desire and worldly things.

Kyle just snapped him silent. "Nope, this is a Mary Magdalene thing."

Before visiting the Red Spring, Kyle wanted to take us to a little chapel down a street called Magdalene Way. Built in 1070, Saint Margaret's Chapel was originally a hospital and almshouse for the poor. It had a sweet little rose garden walled in on either side behind it. And it had these precious, small wooden doors arched at the top like a little hobbit house. We opened the doors and found the chapel empty.

Christiane went so still and solemn as she entered, she was practically floating toward the altar. Kyle, which is why I love him so much, barreled in like a bull in a china shop. He is always, in all circumstances, equal parts pure angel and pure human. I entered last. I was getting that warm, honey feeling, when my heart suddenly feels like a beehive. When there's electricity coursing through me. I knew something crazy was about to happen.

Christiane and Kyle took seats close to each other on the side of the chapel. I followed my body's lead and went to go down on my knees in front of the altar. I closed my eyes. I got still. My legs turned to lead. I felt statuesque. The heaviness, and the stillness, let me drop straight inward, like an anchor. I took a deep breath. And all of a sudden, I could see something I had never noticed before.

I got this tingling sensation, as if a sudden effervescence flooded me, like my blood was now carbonated. Something was happening, for real. Something was releasing through my pores. A belief. A misunderstanding. An ancient fear. That I am safer if I silence myself. That my soul-voice is dangerous. That I am safer if I just hold it here bound within me.

"I have been bound, but I have not bound anything."

The soul in Mary 9:14 is telling us what happens to us from a metaphysical perspective. The soul is bound by the "egoic operating system," by the powers that make us human; fear in all of its manifold forms. The soul, in turn, binds nothing. There's no constriction when it comes to the soul, or, if soul is a stretch for you, then let's say when it comes to love. Only fear binds. And the way that love responds, or the way we can know love is from a sense of expansion, a sense of release.

There's a secret here in this passage that the soul reveals to us. The soul says that it isn't recognized by the powers of the ego. (This is the ego's ignorance, and the binding of our forgetfulness.) But the soul recognizes the seven powers of the ego. And here's the way through: the dissolution of both heaven and earth.

What in the world is the soul talking about here?

We must dissolve our *ideas* of heaven and our *ideas* of earth. We must dissolve the ideas that keep them separate. So that heaven is already here on earth. So that the earth is a heaven we defend and protect. So that we no longer wait, projecting an idea of what's to come, elsewhere, in death, when what is to come is already here. We just haven't recognized it yet.

As we entered the Chalice Well in Glastonbury, where the Red Spring is protected in a walled garden, we walked over a mosaic of the Vesica Pisces made from beautiful white polished stones. This ancient symbol of sacred geometry represents the third that's created from integrating two opposing forces, two seemingly irreconcilable opposites.

There are two circles of equal size and identical shape. And where they overlap creates the most ancient symbol of the divine feminine, the Vesica Pisces. It's an oval, or an egg shape. It's the shape that surrounds Christ in most images and icons of him.

The Vesica Pisces is also on the lid to the well itself. We circled it together and took a soul-family photo like the pilgrims we were. It's one of my favorite photos, ever. We're all lit up like lighthouses. I look at this photo of us and I remember it all. The light that's beaming from our faces tells the story of what love does, how it disarms us, and unbinds us from the chains we placed there ourselves.

Like a Same-Sex Divine Feminine Noah's Ark

I am what anyone can hear but no one can say.

— THE THUNDER, PERFECT MIND 4:23

She reached out both of her arms across our small table in a dimly lit restaurant in Brooklyn. I took Inanna in my hands first. Inanna, the ancient goddess of heaven and earth. She spans the length of Kate's entire forearm. I told her to tell me the story again, of how she felt initiated when she was having the tattoo done. She felt this warmth, a natural numbing sensation every time the tattoo artist touched her forearm to slowly dye her skin with the image of Inanna.

There was a tiny candle on our table, so I turned her arm toward the light to catch more of the glint of gold in the goddess's eyes. Then I reached for her other forearm and held it with both hands. I took in the beauty of this tattoo, which also spanned the length of her forearm. She told me the name of the woman or priestess who adorned this arm, but it didn't sink in. I mean, I heard her say the name, but it seemed to slide through my mind like oil and water.

We had met to talk about an event we were putting together with Eve Ensler, founder of VDAY, titled Just Love, which was a day to heal, gather, and rise together as survivors of sexual assault. So, the name of Kate's second arm tattoo was lost to me as we dove right into the details.

Years later, I was writing the entry for Inanna in the guidebook of *The Divine Feminine Oracle* when I suddenly saw a flash of the tattoo Kate has on her arm opposite to Inanna. I texted her,

"Who's the other lady, not Inanna, on your forearm?"

Within minutes my cell phone dinged: "Enheduanna."

I stared at it. I had to squint to try to figure out how to pronounce it. And then I Googled Enheduanna and nearly fell out of my chair.

She's the human embodiment of the goddess Inanna. The first high priestess. And the first known author in all human history!

So, let me start again.

Long before the spiritual concept of monotheism arrived on the scene, there were many deities, especially female deities, that were celebrated and honored. The goddess Inanna, from the Akkadian Empire, roughly 4500 B.C.E., was worshiped by re-creating the *Hieros gamos*, or the sacred marriage between the divine feminine and the divine masculine.

Inanna's priestesses would choose a consort to reenact the sacred marriage between Inanna and Dumuzi, her male counterpart. The priestesses would ritually make love to their consorts, merging heaven and earth in their bodies, consciously, ritualistically joining the opposites within them as an act of embodying their wholeness.

Enheduanna is an actual historical human woman who lived in roughly 4,200 B.C.E. This was considered in ancient Mesopotamia the pinnacle of Inanna's worship; temples dedicated to Inanna and the priestesses who honored her with their rituals flourished at this time. Enheduanna was the daughter of King Akkad. And she was both spiritually and politically very powerful. She was considered to have reached a semi-divine status in her lifetime.

She is most remembered for her Temple Hymns to Inanna. Hymns that influenced the cadence and poetry of the Psalms in the Old Testament, and the Homeric Epics. Enheduanna is the first known author in all of human history. Her work *The Exaltation of Inanna* has more copies, or inscriptions, than the inscriptions of Kings (which is basically the ancient Mesopotamian version of hitting *The New York Times* bestseller list).

What's significant here to realize is that in some fundamental way, Enheduanna was able to embody the essence of Inanna, which is a force of uniting the light and the dark. The human and the divine. Merging with the shadow, deep beneath the surface of everyday life. Inanna descended to the underworld, or the unconscious, to merge with her "sister" or her twin-shadow-self chained there in the depths to the wall. At each gate, an article of clothing was demanded as her entrance, until at the seventh gate, she was stripped bare. Entirely exposed. And vulnerable.

This is when she meets with her "sister," frees her from the underworld, and rises with her, more powerful than she has ever been before.

Two things hit me like a ton of bricks. First, we are responsible for our own education. History is deeply subjective. There is no master version of history that tells for all of us all the stories we need to hear. The second thing that hit me was a vision that had been sitting on the periphery of my awareness for years. Just waving at me. Wanting me to see it but I just wasn't ready.

So, here's what happened. Because it was very visual and very visceral.

Like a same-sex divine feminine Noah's Ark, I started seeing these divine beings pair up, hand in hand, with these actual human women who lived and breathed and tried their messy best to be their divine counterpart, embodied, while alive.

Here's what I mean. Suddenly, I saw Inanna, naked as all get-out, take the hand of the first writer ever in human history, Enheduanna, Inanna's embodiment. They came together first, I guess, because they felt like the oldest. The first recorded divine-human duo.

Then I saw the Egyptian goddess Isis and Mary Magdalene meet together like Mr. & Ms. Pac-Man before the game begins. First they were face-to-face, and then, facing the same direction, they clasped hands and walked off into the sunset.

Next, I saw the Buddhist goddess Quan Yin and the Chinese princess Miao Shan bow to each other and then walk off together, pinkies linked.

I saw the Tibetan Bodhisattva Vajrayogini loop arms with her reincarnation, Yeshe Tsogyal.

I saw the Celtic goddess of the dawn, Brigid, whistle at and side-eye the Catholic saint Brigid. And on and on . . .

The divine hooking up with the human. What hit me was the clarity I could see that humanity is meant to move the divine story forward.

Let's go back to Isis as an example. The Egyptian goddess Isis dates back to 2,500 B.C.E. and was known for her healing, even resurrecting powers. It's a long story and it has to do with a snake and the sun god Ra, but in brief, Isis secures the power to regenerate life. She's associated with the sexual energy, the life-force that exists within us all and that can be cultivated through meditation and breath-work to promote healing and abundance in our lives.

Like Mary Magdalene, Isis has a partner or consort that is not altogether human: Osiris, the Egyptian god of the afterlife and the dead. And like Christ, Osiris is murdered and his body goes missing. Isis revives his body once it's re-membered. She resurrects him. Just as Mary is the only person there at the tomb, maybe because she had more to do with his ability to come back to life than we've ever recognized.

Maybe because Mary Magdalene is meant to move the story of what it means to be human forward. Or put another way, her story is meant to move a more ancient story of the power of the goddess forward into the modern world. A story of a human woman, a woman in love, who works miracles by bringing love itself back to life.

What I felt like I was witnessing in this divine feminine Noah's Ark was a pairing up of the self with the soul. That we can in a sense die to the individual self and merge with the soul, the love that remains after death. We can become both. So that Isis isn't a goddess in the heavens, but an energy of love that works miracles here in a human heart.

A Religion Every Body Belongs To

When the soul had brought the third Power to naught,
it went upward, and saw the fourth Power. It had seven forms.

— Mary 9:16–17

In France, in 1310, an author named Marguerite Porete was burned at the stake, along with a copy of her book, *The Mirror of Simple Souls*. She was condemned as a "relapsed heretic," and as a free spirit—someone who believed that human beings could achieve union with the divine, without the mediation of the church. Free spirits believed that god is love, and that love (being god) alone could lead the soul to union from within them.

The Mirror of Simple Souls lived on and continued to be translated into other languages and circulated throughout the world. In some ecclesiastical centers, it was considered to be a near-canonical piece of theology, though Marguerite's name had been removed from it. It existed as an anonymous spiritual work until 1946, when Romana Guarnieri identified Latin manuscripts of *The Mirror* in the Vatican. Marguerite Porete's name returned to her book in 1965, when it was published for the first time.

We know very little about Marguerite, except that she was a beguine. Beguines were women who lived in spiritual communities together to live in alignment with Christ's love. They weren't nuns, they never took formal vows; they were always free to come and go. But they lived together with a shared intention to emulate the kind of self-emptying love that Christ mastered. Historians believe she wrote *The Mirror* in Old French sometime between 1296 and 1306. She was deemed a "relapsed heretic" because she was asked by church authorities several times to recant the words she wrote in *The Mirror*. But she refused. Her words were her truth.

The book is structured as a discourse between love and all that is not love, aimed at reaching a state that's indistinguishable from the love that is god. Marguerite leads the reader through the seven stages that her soul ascended through in order to experience this state of union.

And this is what made her work so dangerous. She didn't need the direction of the church, or any external spiritual authority, but rather just the voice of love that existed within her. Marguerite writes in *The Mirror,* "I am God, says Love, for Love is God and God is Love, and this Soul is God by the condition of Love."

Marguerite refers to the liberated soul, the soul that has made it through the seven stages, as a phoenix. This is precisely what her words in *The Mirror* became: they rose from the ashes and took on an immortal life the church could never have anticipated.

Roughly 200 years later, in Spain, Teresa of Avila at the age of 44 began to have a series of visions that convinced her that Christ appeared to her in physical, bodily form, and yet remained invisible to the eye. The sight she had acquired was spiritual.

Teresa had devoted herself to the interior life from an early age. Her childhood was marked by frequent illnesses that confined her to her bed. She read everything she could about spiritual exploration and contemplative prayer. Since she couldn't move or explore the world around her, she went inward. She began to become fluent in the language she heard within her heart, a language of the soul, which includes visions and states of being not ordinarily experienced.

Her visions of Christ lasted for two years and would inform all of her subsequent books, especially her spiritual masterpiece, *The Interior Castle.* Similar to *The Mirror, The Interior Castle* charts the ascent of the soul as an inward journey through the seven mansions or states of being that exist within us. Teresa wanted to share with the other sisters in her Carmelite order the spiritual perception that can be acquired by entering into the seventh mansion where the divine dwells within the soul. She reveals that in the actual moment of union with the divine, the soul feels nothing, but that the divine "removes the scales from its eyes," so that the soul can see at last a "dazzling cloud of light" within the heart.

What's so fascinating to me is that each of these mystics arrives, living in different countries and different centuries, at the same truth: that if we do the spiritual work to allow our soul to pass through the seven stages that exist within us as a part of the human condition, the soul merges with divine love. And the soul is free.

The Gospel of Mary Magdalene was laid buried deep in the Egyptian desert, and hidden in an urn inside a cave, for both Marguerite's and Teresa's lifetimes. They would have never been exposed to the truth it also conveys; that there are seven powers or "climates" the soul must move through to unbind itself from the ego. "Collectively, they comprise the gravitational field of what the contemporary spiritual teacher Thomas Keating has termed "the false self system."[37] They came to it on their own.

If we connect them, if we link them like a forgotten chain, from Mary Magdalene to Marguerite to Teresa, we see a legacy of love being left for us. A trilogy of love stories. And all of them are led by divine love through these seven stages. As if seven is a spiritual truth that exists intrinsically within, encoded in us, like a religion every body belongs to.

Why I Am Proud to Be Part Impala

The first form is darkness; the second is desire; the third is ignorance;
the fourth is zeal for death; the fifth is the realm of the flesh;
the sixth is the foolish wisdom of the flesh;
and the seventh is the wisdom of the wrathful person.
These are the seven powers of wrath.

— Mary 9:18–25

The definition of a pilgrimage is simply a journey to a sacred place as a demonstration of devotion. What compels us to become so devoted that we're willing to leave home for weeks, even months at a time, and travel halfway around the world, away from family, and loved ones, in order to reach this sacred place—that is a more complex mystery.

All I can say is that I wish it wasn't compulsory. But it is, or it has been for me. And this has posed immense challenges. Because I have the constitution of a cloistered nun. I don't travel well. Okay, that's a massive understatement. I am one of the world's worst travelers. I am that anxious, sweaty, ugly-crying mess next to you when the plane hits turbulence. I am that backseat driver pointing out a sharp curve in the road up ahead to the bus driver. I can't relax on anything that moves.

I was asked to speak at an event in the South of France (which then meant I could finally visit Mary Magdalene's cave) and I was asked to give a workshop based on my first book, *REVEAL,* in Devon, England (which then meant I could visit Glastonbury again and the Red and White Spring).

So even though, as always, I just wanted to remain in my cozy apartment, take care of my sweet little man, and stay the hell still, I said yes. I said yes because I heard a yes, if you know what I mean. I didn't think about it, or listen to the way my ego took off and started panicking; I felt the yes. It was sitting there inside me like the only grown-up in a room filled with toddlers.

Moving "home" to Cleveland meant that I no longer had to keep moving. I didn't have to be subject to the whims and greed of landlords raising rent beyond my means. I could own my apartment. I could make a new beginning as an indie mom, a life that looked a lot more like thriving rather than just surviving.

But moving "home" to Cleveland also meant coming face-to-face with all the reasons why it never felt like home to me. The assault I experienced as a little girl at a friend's house, and the inability to sleep for years after, or feel safe at night, or fly without sheer panic and dread.

It was all still here, waiting for me, when I returned. And with those memories came a panic disorder, because the body never lies, and the body never forgets.

I had already talked my way through years of therapy. And I was grateful for the clarity it gave me. But this return demonstrated to me that I had never healed all the way down and all the way through. I had managed. I had found ways to cope with the anxiety and fear that coursed through me most of the time, every day. I practiced the soul-voice meditation, I did yoga, or walked, or danced, or hula-hooped. I found a way every day to express the excess energy so that it wasn't harnessed for a panic attack.

And I chanted the prayer of the heart that Penny had taught me. Whenever the panic started to course through my veins in a way that made me certain I was about to leave my body altogether, I chanted from an intercom in my heart, *"Lord Jesus Christ son of god have mercy on me."*

Mary 9:18's full list of the seven powers that exist within us for me is both the most humbling and the most helpful for being human. It reads like an ingredients label of the ego. It's not suggesting that we all contain each of these elements in equal measure. But if we can understand it, it's giving us an informative list of the powers of the ego that can potentially for hours, days, years at a time hold us captive.

The first is darkness. I experience this as heaviness, depression, that feeling of being trapped, or constricted. That sensation that things suck, and they will always suck. That there isn't a light at the end of the tunnel, there's just more tunnel. Helpless. Hopeless. And thinking I'm alone.

The second is desire, or as Cynthia Bourgeault translates it, craving. For me, desire or craving is clinging. Wishing things could have been different. (I get seduced by this power frequently.) Attachment to what I think I want (which is usually light-years away from what I actually need). This is essentially wanting to be where I am not.

The third is ignorance. This comes in the form of my lack of awareness. This is when I'm unconscious about something. And sometimes we need to be unconscious. It's important to make clear that this "ignorance" isn't an indication of a deficit of character or intelligence. It can actually be integral to healing. We can only see so much at once. We sometimes need to open our awareness about an aspect of ourselves, or an event that happened in our lives, in increments. And this is actually wise. The ignorance Mary is talking about is different; it's about the unconscious states we can fall into, and then act from.

The fourth is zeal for death. Or the craving for death. This sounds exceptionally odd. It later becomes, within Christianity's "Seven Deadly Sins," the sin of gluttony. Also a strange and rarely used word, but easier to understand. It's about making choices in our lives that endanger our health or impair our longevity. Eating, drinking, and having sex in ways that neglect and harm the body. So, to be clear, it's not that attending to the body or indulging in anything that gives us pleasure is a "sin" or a power of the ego. ("There is no such thing as sin.") It's when we do this to an extreme that actually harms the body. It's that human tendency in us to be destructive toward the body. To take our pain out on the least-deserving possible thing, our own body. This is where the ego can take us, if we're lost in this power and we've completely forgotten the soul.

The fifth is the realm of the flesh. Or enslavement to the physical body. This to me is when we're entirely identified with being a body, and only a body. It's the power that's later defined as lust, but I think it's important to distinguish something. Lustful people are my favorite humans to encounter. I feel more alive around them. I had a boyfriend who could eat a meal in a way that made me jealous of everything on his plate. He lusted after his food. He lusted after my body in the same passionate way. And it was bliss. Lust, for me at least, isn't the issue. It's our relationship to it. Does it derail us almost entirely from our work, or does it fuel and inspire it? Does it harm the people we love, or does it light them up (like my boyfriend's lust lit me up)? For me, as a woman, as a survivor, it's a triumph to be lustful, to be present in my body during sex. It's an uncelebrated victory. Where the fifth power can trip us up is when we forget that we are also a soul, not just this passionate body with its fiery needs. And it most explicitly applies to when that lust includes a sacrilegious transgression of forcing our physical needs on someone who does not consent to them.

The sixth is the foolish wisdom of the flesh. Or the false peace of the flesh. This power later comes to be referred to as sloth. This one took me the longest to unpack. First of all, I'm insanely in love with sloths. Actual sloths. My son and I watch nonstop *Animal Planet* videos of baby sloths doing just about anything, and we melt. We've even perfected the baby-sloth cry. So, sloth does nothing for me in terms of understanding a power of the ego. And then second, this original description from Mary's gospel as the foolish wisdom of the flesh, this trips me up as well.

I think it has taken us a long time to understand that the body is wise. The body has been manipulated and vilified for millennia as the scapegoat for our own vices. It has taken the sexual revolution and the feminist movement to reclaim the body. To understand that we can trust the body to take us to realms of pleasure and joy that don't have to be separate from our spirituality or religion. That we can trust the body when it comes to nutrition and craving foods that we need or that just bring us pleasure (when we are not in a cycle of addiction). That we can trust the body when it comes to alerting us to a dangerous situation or person. That we can trust the body to make us aware of needing to slow down, or decrease our stress levels. That we can trust the body to heal. That we can trust the body is more than just a machine to use, and misuse, at the ego's whim. That we can trust the body has wisdom the intellect can never grasp, like the way a woman's body forms another body within her even as she sleeps. That we can trust the body to tell us who we feel at home with. If we know how to listen, the body has wisdom, blood memory, that reaches back through the centuries and carries the echoes of our ancestors.

What this sixth power has come to mean to me is that there is a reticence to change, a reluctance to do what we know is best for us, and we can feel this viscerally in the body. There's a sluggishness, a tendency toward inertia. If we are headed to the couch the second we get home from work, that routine will be arduous to break. The body becomes easily habituated, meaning the routines we create can become engrained in us. The body is so loyal. And if we develop patterns of inaction, we will have to contend with a body that doesn't really want to do anything.

The seventh power is the power we all probably understand and know most intimately. The seventh power in the Gospel of Mary is the wisdom of the wrathful person. Or the compulsion of rage. It almost sounds like Christ, or Mary, since Christ is the one who originally gave this list to Mary, is being sardonic. Right? If this is a power of the ego, a power that keeps us from knowing our true self, then how could a wrathful person be wise?

For me, similar to the power of lust, or the realm of the flesh, anger is healing. To feel and express my anger feels healthy. Anger creates appropriate boundaries with people who aren't supporting us or who aren't good for us to be around. Anger can flood the system with a sense of clarity and purpose. We sometimes know what we stand for and what we care most about from the presence of anger. Anger protects us and often protects others we love and those who can't defend themselves. Anger, for anyone who has been silenced or made to feel insignificant, is a declaration that they actually matter. That their voice matters. That they are not to be silenced ever again. Anger in these situations is holy. Anger in the face of injustice is an act of love. It's a statement of unifying ourselves with a stranger and saying, "I won't let you be treated as I would not want to be treated myself." Anger can be motivating and unifying. As the mystic William Blake relates, "The voice of honest indignation is the voice of god."

And also, anger can devour us from the inside out. Anger can divide. It is so compelling, it can derail and distract many of us for most of our lives. And this is how I think we can best understand the destructive side of anger; it's simply when we get overcome by it. We can live in anger, or we can act on our anger in ways that we will regret then for the rest of our lives.

As with all the powers, it isn't the power itself that's harmful. It's the presence of the power and the absence of the soul. It's forgetting entirely that we are not just the ego that is subject to the power. So, even as we are more enraged than we have ever been (even if we have every right to be, and it's healthy and normal for us to be so angry), if we forget that there's this equally significant part of us that is calm, still water beneath it all, then we will inflict our rage onto someone else. And whether that person is undeserving of that rage or in our eyes "deserving" of it, all it does is bind us to that person and to perpetuate a cycle of rage.

As the brilliant comedian Hannah Gadsby relates about her sexual assault in *Nanette*, "I have a right to be angry, but not to spread it." We know that hurt people hurt people. And this is a source of compassion we can access when we need relief from our anger. But ultimately, this seventh power is about the responsibility we need to take for the rage that can compel us to treat ourselves and others in ways we can hardly believe we're capable of. I think it's the seventh because it's the hardest to come to terms with. How do we responsibly express our rage? How do we let anger motivate and mobilize us without burning us out or burning the house down?

And anger is the seventh, I think, also because it's often the reason we become more vulnerable to the other six powers of ego. We're angry at the person who has harmed us and so we fall into a depression, or we cling obsessively to what could have been, or we harm ourselves physically by overeating or drinking or taking drugs in an effort to deal with that rage. And it's just a tangled, gritty mess. And we feel trapped.

So, on the one hand, it's daunting to take in all seven powers at once. Holy crap, look at what we have to contend with, look at all the derailing powers that we contain. And yet, on the other hand, it feels like such a relief. Like, welcome to being human. This is normal, you binge watching Netflix to forget your pain, you drinking red wine like it's a secret elixir for all fears, you sobbing over a divorce that happened seven years ago, you angry at what happened to you as a little girl and enraged anytime you ever hear of it happening to anyone else. You. Human being. You. Welcome. You're not alone. You're not odd, or strange, or actually different at all. You're meant to feel all these things. And none of these feelings, these powers, make you less holy. They connect you. They make you, you. And this is part of the whole point of being here. To feel these horrible and hard derailing things, and to find your way back to love.

So, this time when the anxiety disorder came back, I was armed with the road map of my own humanity that Mary's gospel had given me. It gave me the perspective to notice these powers rear up and get louder, and to know that they're nothing to be ashamed of or afraid of or to judge. I can be depressed. And angry. I can. I am human. And I can choose to use the presence of each of these powers as an opportunity to learn to strengthen my capacity to return to love.

A close friend of mine suggested EMDR (Eye Movement Desensitization and Reprocessing). She had recently remembered a childhood sexual assault and found that this form of therapy was powerful because it released the trauma that was still trapped there in the body. I found a therapist and began work three months before my pilgrimage to Mary Magdalene.

Trauma lives in the body in present tense. And many, many illnesses stem from that truth. Because the body, as our most faithful warrior, will hold for us what we can't face ourselves. Until we live into the strength to go all the way back, and experience it for the first time, long after it has actually happened.

My body had waited for me, all these years, to return now that I'm filled with a fierce love that flows through me as much and as often as I can remember that it does. Now that I'm home in my body, my beloved body can give back to me what it has held for me for all these years.

During a particularly powerful session, my therapist told me a story. (And his stories were always medicine, told with intention.) It went something like this:

A cheetah is stalking a herd of impala. As if one unified and entirely connected mass, the herd senses the cheetah at the same moment and begins to flee at top speed. A young impala falters and gets delayed just for a split second. But that's enough time for the cheetah to pounce. At the moment of contact, the impala falls to the ground, as if instantly struck dead. But it isn't. And it isn't pretending to be dead either. It has fallen into an instinctive and involuntary altered state of consciousness shared by all mammals when death appears imminent.

Physiologists call this state the immobility state or the freezing response. The other two responses to extreme situations of impending doom are fight and flight. These two states are very well known and researched. But this third state is less known, and little is understood about this altered state of immobility.

But nature has developed it for two main reasons. First, it serves as a last-ditch effort to survive. The impala in its altered state is dragged back to a tree in the shade. In thinking the impala is dead, the cheetah is not on the alert. So, with its guard down, while turning its back, the impala can leap up, shake off the effects of the immobility response, and escape.

The second reason is that while in this altered state the impala can't feel any pain. It's a prehistoric function developed so that in our last moments we die before we're even killed.

It is not under our conscious control. It's about energy and the nervous system. Humans and animals share this same capacity to play possum. The difference is that the impala can simply shake off the experience to release the energy of the trauma without a story line or subsequent symptoms.

Humans, though, especially with this third response to trauma, can develop PTSD and anxiety disorders from the energy of the "death" being trapped in the body.

Trauma expert Peter Levine in *Waking the Tiger* explains that "this residual energy does not simply go away. It persists in the body, and often forces the formation of a wide variety of symptoms."[38]

I had always thought of "fight or flight," as at least doing something. This third option, "freeze," had always felt like a failure to me. Freeze felt passive, or worse, it felt cowardly.

I had tears streaming down my face. It was all beginning to make sense, because I was beginning to understand what was keeping me from healing (all the way back and all the way through).

I had never been able to reconcile the feisty, brave, and precocious girl I was before the assault and then the fact that I didn't fight, didn't scream, didn't even move. I wept as my therapist reached for the tissues and set them gently beside me.

I had been haunted by this unease of not knowing why I didn't protect myself. There was a part of me that never trusted myself in the same way again, with that same level of ease and love.

I had lost a lot that night, the greatest of which was this unfaltering belief in myself.

Now I understood. I did fight back. I froze. I froze because I ardently believed I wouldn't survive that assault. I died before I could be killed. I froze because the animal instinct in me kicked in, and it saved me from having to experience the pain.

I did exactly what I was supposed to. I hadn't failed. I had saved my own life.

How the Long Island Medium Answered My Prayer

They interrogated the soul, "Where are you coming from, human-killer, and where are you going, space-conqueror?"

— MARY 9:26

Remember when Princess Fiona in *Shrek* finally gets her true love kiss?

She lifts into the air in a mystical fog of radiant light, rays shooting out of the palms of her hands and the soles of her feet. We assume that, when the fog clears, and she's placed back down on the ground of the cathedral, she will be the lithe, sinewy Fiona she was in the daylight. We trust that true love morphs her permanently into the physical form she loved most.

So, at first, we feel shocked along with her as she takes in her still huge green hands, and her bulky ogre feet. But then she locks eyes with Shrek, and she sees his expression shift from surprise to wonder and then to pure, melted light. We see that she gets it. She gets that the real transformation comes in letting love reach within her where it hasn't before.

It doesn't come from turning into the form that her ego wants, or that others might have preferred for her to be. It's not about making more sense from the outside. It's about bringing what she had kept hidden, what she only revealed at night, what she kept secret as the thing that was most hideous about her, and returning it to the light.

When I had a three-day panic attack from trying to book my flights to Europe for the pilgrimage, I felt a lot like Fiona. I was shocked and not a little bit horrified to see that this level of fear still lived in me.

I thought I had overcome my fear of flying. I was flying, not comfortably, not without grabbing the hand of whoever happened to be next to me and leaving red marks from the strength of the grip I needed to not lose it during takeoff, turbulence, landing—basically the whole flight. I was flying, but not without a glass of red wine, and sometimes a sedative, and sometimes both.

I meditated after the fear returned until my back was sore. I lassoed my soul to tell me something reassuring. I sobbed. And at the end of it all, I finally asked for guidance. (I seem to only reach spiritual surrender via exhaustion.) So, I went inward. I took a deep breath to descend into the heart. I took a second, deeper breath once there, and felt a calm come over me. I asked, "What is this anxiety wanting me to see?" "What do I still need to learn from this panic disorder?"

I heard, saw, and felt absolutely nothing. I blamed the level of anxiety I was experiencing. I waited. I asked again, "Why has this anxiety returned?" Again, crickets. But I've been meditating for long enough now that silence doesn't upset me. I rested in it for a while and then took the third deep, intentional breath that lets me open my eyes again, now from a place more rooted back into my heart.

As I walked into the living room the next morning, my son had somehow cued up an episode of *The Long Island Medium* and resumed where it had been paused just as I sat down next to him. I inhaled the smell of his hair, I held his adorable form, gathering as much of him and his long legs as I could in my arms, and I whispered, "Good morning, lovedove."

He shushed me, and pointed at the TV. Theresa Caputo was describing how her phobias used to keep her confined to her house. Her fear of being in a car, or of even just leaving the house, became so great that at one point her family had to help with her grocery shopping. She was agoraphobic at the height of her anxiety, not able to go anywhere. I got that weird warm feeling as she spoke as if my heart was suddenly pumping honey. I listened really closely then, as if my ears were turning up their capacity to receive sound, as if they could zero in like Superman and hear a pin drop three stories down.

The Long Island Medium went on to explain then that the panic attacks were actually moments when spirit was trying to reach through to her. But she wasn't listening. The anxiety was like spirit banging pots and pans trying to get her attention. Once she began to listen inward, to receive messages, the anxiety lifted.

I teared up. First, because this was clearly the answer to the question I had asked in my heart. And second, my son had been the one to gift it to me.

I understood then that I was judging the panic attack, as if it was a bad thing. As if it was a step back. As if it wasn't just more light trying to reach through to me. As if healing is ever linear.

I understood the opportunity I had in this moment. I could treat this fear with the love I never gave it in the past. I judged it. I was ashamed of it. I tried to hide it and medicate it. I treated myself as "special," meaning broken. I felt damaged because of it. I called it names, as the threatened ego always does whenever we try to free ourselves: *"human-killer, space-conqueror."*

In this moment, though, I understood the fear as a form of communication. As a message that there's so much more support I can receive. I understood it as a chance to be compassionate to this place in me that's so terrified to fly. I could let love reach where it hasn't been before. I could let love marry the ogre and the princess inside me.

And that's how I ended up on a boat to Europe for my pilgrimage to Mary Magdalene. A boat named the *Queen Mary*. (Of course.)

Sometimes the most loving thing to do doesn't appear to be the bravest. It's not about pushing through or overpowering fear. Sometimes we just need to be with where we are terrified. And not ask the terror to leave or change. But dare to become the one who can hold it in a love that didn't exist before it, a love that grew, and expanded in order to meet it.

THE FOURTH POWER

CRAVING FOR DEATH

A Ship Without Sails

1) TAKE A SELFIE DURING THE FIRE DRILL: There's a mandatory fire drill before leaving port that everyone on board has to take part in. That's everyone, all 2,000 passengers and 1,000 officers and staff. You'll be divided into muster stations, which just means the place where you go if there's a fire as we're crossing the ocean. You'll have to be in your life jacket. It's very large, very orange, and you'll most likely be sweating. You'll be crammed into an odd room, like the cafeteria, or the casino, and one of the officers will be explaining what happens if the worst happens. (Sort of like a flight attendant as the plane is taxiing down the runway toward takeoff.) You'll be a bit green, if like me, you get dizzy from being on rocking objects, surrounded by more people than most people can manage to be around, and all while wearing a life jacket that keeps reminding you that you're about to be out where there is no land, in any direction, for seven days. Take a selfie just before you go into a full-blown panic attack. (And obviously, never show it to anyone.) This is the photo you will cherish for the rest of your life. It's that priceless.

2) NEVER CROSS THE OCEAN ALONE: No one does. And I'm not being dramatic. This is a fact. No one signs up to cross the ocean by boat for seven days completely on her own. That is, except me. Or let me say this another way. If you cross the ocean alone, just be forewarned that everyone does everything in pairs, and everyone on board expects you to be with a partner, or your family, or at least your elderly mother. No one will even be able to comprehend what the hell you're doing all alone crossing the ocean on a boat. So, just prepare yourself for the stares, the awkward moments of silence, and the incomprehension as people you meet try to take in that you're actually single and solo on the ship.

3) BRING A BATTERY-OPERATED CANDLE: And keep it lit. Because, guess what, the path that the ship takes to cross the Atlantic from New York to Southampton, England, passes over the mass grave of the *Titanic*. Yep. And it's the most bone-haunting moment you'll ever witness. And yep, it happens in the middle of the night. And you'll know about it ahead of time, you'll know to stay up terrified until the ship has passed over it, because everyone on board will be talking about it, and by everyone, I mean the people you're assigned to eat with for every meal. They are your lifeline. (That is, if you didn't heed my advice and you find yourself alone on the *Queen Mary*.) Your dining crew and your candle: these are your tethers to staying calm. And by staying calm, I just mean, appearing normal. Keep the candle lit at all times. Even during the day. It infuses it with this supernatural power to be this steady light, this one constant, as the days pass, and the sea swells become the new ground beneath you. It's there with you, like Wilson was there for Tom Hanks's character in *Castaway*. And listen, don't panic if it switches off when the ship passes over the final resting place of the Titanic, as it did for me. Just calmly switch it back on, and say a prayer from the sudden humility you feel, being so small, and helpless, and human, aware of the fathoms extending out beneath you.

4) PAY CLOSE ATTENTION TO YOUR DREAMS: You know how when you've visited the ocean, slept near it, or spent some time walking alongside it, letting the waves race over your feet, or taking time to look out over the horizon, letting your mind try to imagine if there's anything more beautiful, more ancient and endless, letting yourself feel the pure expansion from just taking in deeper and deeper breaths of that briny air—then you dream like a lunatic? Well, just imagine how amped up your dreaming gets if you're not sleeping *next* to the ocean but *on* it! It's like an experiment in being human, to be out there where no human can actually exist for very long without fresh water and something to float on. You are, yourself, your body, at an interstice. You're between landmasses. You're out there (beyond your depths) at the mercy of the sea (and this ship that's the length of the Empire State Building). So, trust me, even if you haven't dreamed in years, or even if you're someone who wakes up and sort of vaguely remembers a few details but then loses it all as soon as you get out of bed, even if you don't have an interest in dreams and what they tell us, pay close attention to them. Write them down. (You'll have time.) And save it. Like the selfie at your muster station before the ship left port. Keep it like a pearl the sea gave you. Don't share it with anyone. Not if you don't want to.[39]

5) YOU WILL HAVE A WILD CRUSH ON THE CAPTAIN: It will not be rational. It will not be something you tell anyone at your dining table. But you will have a wild crush on the captain. No matter how old he is, and no matter your sexual orientation. He will become that god you always said never existed, the one that has a beard and speaks to you in this Old Testament, disembodied voice. And you will trust and believe absolutely everything he says. Which will be at noon, exactly, every day of the crossing. You'll look forward to his daily updates like the faithful await a Sunday sermon. You'll even hush the people around you who are somehow unaware that god is on the intercom. He'll let you know precisely, in longitude and latitude, where you are in the crazy blue that stretches in every direction for as far as you can see. He'll

let you know where, on that particular day, the nearest landmass is, which will feel both comforting and terrifying at the exact same time. He will give you odd bits of maritime history or otherworldly comments about the sea, like how at that very moment you're passing over a mountain range, and even after he signs off for the day, you'll remain in the very spot you were standing or sitting when he began his daily talk, letting that visual overpower you and all your senses, taking in this reality that only the alchemists reached: as above, so below. You'll see the hull of the ship and let your mind travel for leagues until you see them, the tips of the mountain range, the peaks that miraculously exist down there.

6) CROSS YOURSELF INCESSANTLY: Personally, I can never remember if I'm supposed to go to the left or the right first after touching the third-eye area of the forehead. I fumble it up every time. So, if you know how to cross yourself, and it's something that works for you, lean into it. If you don't, or if you're like me and you get your wires crossed when you try to employ it, just do something, anything, that lets you bless yourself when you feel something fortunate happen when you're at sea. Some examples: I don't know what the chances would be, slim to nonexistent, that I would know anyone on board (unless, of course, I had invited them). But not only did I know someone on board, I was seated right next to him at my assigned dining table: table number one. He's one of the best friends of my best friend, Donna. We had met (without remembering it) seven years before when I gave the blessing at Donna's wedding. He was crossing with his mother for a milestone birthday. Every time we talked about writing (he's an author) or every time he came to my defense when the three fates would cross-examine me (I'll talk about them next), I wanted to cross myself. So I said the prayer of the heart instead. Or when *Jane Eyre* came on in French, to my relief, when I couldn't sleep after my little candle went off right as we crossed the mass grave of the Titanic. I went straight into the prayer of the heart, on repeat. Or when the quiet, middle-aged man from Devon, sitting with his wife to the other side of me at the dining table, suddenly cut off

the table's conversation to tell us all about a program he saw on Mary Magdalene. And we all stared at him at first like he might be possessed or having some sort of out-of-body experience, because he rarely spoke, much less commanded the attention of the entire table. And then he told us how he had turned up the volume on the telly (*love* that word) when he realized the program about Mary Magdalene was focused on the debate about whether or not she was really a prostitute. I asked him what he thought of it; he shook his head and said he had fallen asleep halfway through it. But it stuck with him, the debate about who she was. I recited the prayer of the heart right then, too. Because in the moment while he was talking about Mary, and while we were all held rapt, I knew why I was away from my little man, why despite my fear of the return flight, I knew I was doing what I had to do. I had to visit Mary Magdalene's cave. I was exactly where I was supposed to be. And that felt like a blessing.

7) IF FATE ASKS YOU FOR A DRINK, SAY YES: At first, fate didn't know what to make of me. What was a single mum doing out on holiday by herself. (In other, clearer words, what kind of selfish, shit mum is this?) This is the judgment, and the line of questioning, that my writer friend would help me deflect from fate every evening when I had to face them. They will cross the sea with you, so just be prepared to meet with them. They are destiny personified. There are three of them. And they're all from Surrey. They've known each other for their entire lives and can practically speak in eyebrow. They know each other's thoughts before they each can think them. They are intimidating and hysterical to be around. And if they ask you out for a drink, just say yes. I said no every night, mostly because you can take the hermit out of her cozy apartment but you can't take the hermit out of the hermit even if you throw her out to sea. And also because I had misinterpreted the theme of death that kept creeping up in pretty much everything I tried to do. For example, the Shakespeare Theatre Company from London was performing *all* the death scenes from the classics throughout the crossing. And the only music I happened

to go hear, when I forced myself to go do something other than stare at the sea in awe, turned out to be a funeral march from New Orleans. It was the music of death as a celebration, a victory even. Death as the one thing we've actually never needed to fear. So, I was mistaken in sort of taking heed because of this death theme on board with us. I should have known that it was about Mary Magdalene. That there's a love that's stronger than death, and this is what I had made myself a pilgrim to know. So, I didn't go out with them until the last night. It was the night of the masquerade in the Queens Room. Gillian, Jackie, and Lilly were dressed to the nines. Set for mingling with the decadence and gluttony. We had an issue with finding the right table. We started at one in the back corner, but Lilly felt we needed to be closer to the dance floor to get chosen. She loves to "pull," the other two fates told me while laughing. "Pull" is British for attracting men (I think). So, we went to a large table with a velvet booth toward the front of the ballroom. An elderly couple was already sitting there, giving us the stink eye as we joined them. Lilly somehow knocked the table as she was trying to sit down and spilled a healthy splash of the elderly man's lager right onto his lap. The man's wife was immediately outraged. And started yelling at Gillian, who didn't even realize what Lilly had done. Gillian took the brunt of it, though, and got out a tissue (a used one, she later told me). The couple was absolutely incensed and unforgiving. The elderly wife was so worked up, she finally shouted, "Just leave!" The three fates looked at each other, then at me, and we all broke out into hysterics. So we left. And slowly made our way back to the table in the corner where we had started.

I couldn't stop laughing. Lilly pulled, and I laughed again, as she looked back at us just before she reached the dance floor with this smile of sheer triumph. It felt so good to laugh at everything, like it was a superpower the three fates were reminding me of that I had forgotten. Laugh at the absurd, they whispered. Everything passes. All the details, they fade. But what fate, or destiny, and the ocean have in common is the surrender that's offered to you.

When water is all you can see on the horizon in all directions, for seven days, the soul sees itself in it. The soul feels recognized. It is as vast as this. There's this acute awareness that the soul is this presence of love within us; and that no matter what, this is what can never be lost. The only death is the one of who you had been before. Or who you thought you were. And you realize now that this is a blessing. To get to die while still living.

The Yoni of the Mountain

The companion [koinonos] of the Son is Miriam of Magdala.
The Teacher loved her more than all the disciples;
he often kissed her on the mouth.

— The Gospel of Philip

The first man I met in Paris was a tall vagina. His costume went from his shoulders to below his knees, and included some very accurate anatomy. And judging from his bare arms and legs, it seemed to be the only thing he was wearing. He was just sauntering through the Gare du Nord as if in normal attire. The man-vagina was with two other men, so when I tried to take a picture of him, they beckoned for me to come join them. Then one of them offered to take a picture of us. So, that became one of my favorite pictures of my pilgrimage to Mary Magdalene's cave. Me cracking up in Paris standing next to a man wearing nothing but a full-length vagina.

I was headed down to Aix-En-Provence from Paris to have dinner with a woman I had never met before. Rose had sent a message to me through Instagram shortly before I got on the *Queen Mary*. And typically, I don't reply to these messages. But her profile picture showed a red thread on her left wrist. So I read it. She said that she had moved to the South of France with her daughters for the past year in order to be close to Mary Magdalene, both her cathedral in Saint-Maximin and her cave at Sainte-Baume. She suggested we meet for dinner in Aix, which is the closest city to Saint-Maximin. It felt important that I meet her, but I didn't know why yet.

I needed to get from the Gare du Nord to the Gare de Lyon to catch a train to Aix in Southern France. I went to stand in the taxi line and an English woman arrived in line behind me. She told me that she was late to catch a train, the only one, headed to Barcelona from Gare de Lyon.

I suggested we split a cab, and her face lit up. She helped me lift our bags and myself over the gate and out of the line. We got in the cab and started talking. Then my face lit up when she said she was from Devon. I told her about the workshop I was holding in Devon later that month. We hugged at the station after she helped me get my ticket to Aix. I felt drenched in this sense of how magical it can feel to be led from one synchronicity to the next.

Rose was waiting for me outside of my hotel. And before I could even introduce myself, we started laughing. We had both noticed that we were wearing the exact same Mary Magdalene medallion. She felt immensely familiar to me.

We walked slowly through the sand-colored buildings and the gorgeous light that seemed to thicken the air. It felt like we were walking through an invisible warm bath, as we wove our way through the maze of narrow streets to a bistro in an alleyway filled with brightly painted shutters and flower boxes. As we waited for the food to arrive, we started sharing what being devoted to Mary Magdalene has taught us.

There's scriptural evidence in the Gospel of Philip that Mary was referred to as his companion, or *koinonos* in Greek. This word can translate as married partner, counterpart, beloved, companion in faith. The fact that Philip goes on to relate that not only is Mary Christ's *koinonos*, but that "he loved her more than all the disciples," and that "he often kissed her on the mouth," suggests that their partnership was also physical.

Whether they were ever sexually united or not, for me, is less important than the fact that they were a couple, a duo, partners. That they were meant to be seen together, understood as a whole. That maybe part of Christ's teachings could only be completed with and through her. What feels most important to me is that we've forgotten and willfully buried this aspect of Christ, that he was in love with Mary.

Rose and I agreed that what this has meant for us spiritually—to have a belief in Mary as singularly significant to Christ that isn't validated on an institutionalized level—is that we have to validate this belief for ourselves. We've had to become fierce about recognizing what's true for us. And we both felt as though this is something that our devotion to Mary Magdalene has asked of us personally. We've needed to learn to believe in ourselves, in our own voice, in what we know is true, even if the world around us does not confirm this truth for us. Cultivating a sense of self-worth seems to be a compulsory part of the spiritual path of Mary Magdalene. Because we cannot believe in ourselves if we don't remember that we are worthy of that belief.

It felt good to be in communion with another woman who understands Mary as I do. And to be with someone who has dedicated her life to her in the same way.

Her red thread kept catching my eye as she lifted her water glass for a drink. *We remember her,* it seemed to whisper. And now, we're remembering each other. As if we're circling back up, coming from out of hiding, out of the wilderness and into the clearing. Now, we can remember her together.

I had a steady, assembly-line-like flow going of picking up a french fry, dunking it into mayo, and then hauling it into my mouth as we talked. But when Rose suddenly mentioned the Cave of Eggs, a mayo-tipped fry halted abruptly midair. My jaw dropped.

"The Cave of Eggs?!" I said as both a question and an exclamation. Because at first it didn't feel real. That it could exist. That my obsession with Mary Magdalene's connection to the egg could be validated by a secret, mystical cave I had never even heard of before.

"It's a place for the initiated," Rose said. "Not everyone finds it." Then she showed me a picture of it and I could see why. This cave was clearly the yoni of the mountain. Its entrance was a rock version of a Georgia O'Keefe painting. Pure rose-petal folds of stone lined a dark opening.

This is why I had come on the pilgrimage. Not to go to the cave the church has created in her honor at Sainte-Baume, as I had thought—the one I had heard about at Saintes-Maries-de-la-Mer almost 20 years before. I was here to find this secret cave. The Cave of Eggs.

What I Heard in Mary Magdalene's Crypt

The soul replied, saying, "What binds me has been slain, and what surrounds me has been destroyed, and my desire has been brought to an end, and ignorance has died."

— Mary 9:27

The Mary Magdalene basilica in Saint-Maximin in the South of France sits back from a small medieval road built in the center of town. There's a large square made of smooth, beautiful stone that stretches out before the entrance. When I passed through the doors, I didn't feel like an intruder or an outsider, as I usually do. It felt like if there was ever a church where I belonged, it would be this basilica where Mary Magdalene is most revered, and most remembered.

Rose was waiting outside to let me have time alone, to explore the church. She had driven me from Aix to this small village in Saint-Maximin. And then she'd helped translate for me at Le Couvent Royale, a convent turned hotel that's attached to Mary Magdalene's church. She explained to the receptionist that I wanted a small room that faced the church courtyard and that I would need a ride to her cave at Sainte-Baume in the morning. Rose's face was glowing as she said all this. She was so small and powerful. She reminded me of Sarah-La-Kali, the patron saint of the gypsies, Queen of the Outsiders. Her devotion radiated off her skin. Her hand gestures to accompany her eloquent French were quick and graceful, almost hummingbird-like.

The temperature fell nearly 20 degrees inside the cathedral. It was in the upper 90s outside. This region of France is sunny for the majority of the entire year, and in the summer months, there's a steady, unrelenting golden light that pours down onto the bright ancient design of Saint-Maximin. The church with its thick stone somehow traps the cooler air, and its protection from the sun comes as sanctuary.

There was a tall plastic Christ on a pedestal near the entrance to Mary Magdalene's crypt. It was the kind that didn't give me the creeps. Christ is pointing gently to his sacred heart blazing in the center of his chest. He's in a red and gold toga outfit. And his one foot is bare and exposed beneath his robe as if he's taking a step forward. I watched as an elderly couple approached him. They each kissed their fingertips and then placed their hands lovingly on his foot. It was a gesture I was certain they made very often together, maybe every day.

Once they moved on, I stood so that his downcast gaze met me eye to eye. I had an earache and a slight fever. The three fates had been convinced I got it from all the swimming I did in the ship's pool. As far as I could remember, I had never had an earache before. I kept assuming it would just go away, but it had gotten worse. I was dabbing some eucalyptus oil around my ears each morning to try to pull out the water. It made me smell bizarre, like a walking throat lozenge. I tried throughout the day plugging my nose and blowing out the pressure trapped there in my ears, but nothing had helped. It still sounded like I was underwater. Or holding my breath.

I noticed the stigmata in Christ's foot. This is what the couple must have kissed. I knew then that this life-sized statue was meant to represent the risen Christ. I pressed my fingertips to my lips and touched his lacquered-cement toes. I knew if anyone was watching, they would know instantly that I had never kissed Christ's foot before.

I descended into the crypt then, with my eau de Vick's VapoRub following in a waft behind me. There are several even, polished steps that lead to the entrance. There's an alabaster statue behind glass of Mary Magdalene reclining with her head tilted back as if hearing something that has overcome or overwhelmed her. Her eyes are closed, as if she's listening intently within.

Then there are several uneven stone steps that lead down into the crypt itself, clearly marking a more ancient part of the cathedral. It was even colder in the crypt. As I descended, I noticed that people had etched messages in the wall. The writing was an almost neon-white set against the dark stone. What caught my eye was a large *M + C* drawn within a heart. Sacred graffiti. I smiled. Then I ducked my head, held the rickety metal railing, and took the final three steps down. I tried to make sense of this odd-looking gate at the back of the crypt. I had to really squint and focus to see what was caged behind it.

At first I thought it was some sort of scary golden eagle with a skull face. I got as close to it as I could and realized then that the golden wings weren't from a bird but an angel. There were four golden angels holding up her skull from each corner. And the skull was wrapped in red cloth. I could just see the edges of it framing her skull in red. There was this odd, see-through glass bubble that protected it.

The skull has been sealed inside this case since 1974. What is scientifically known about the skull is that it's the skull of a female who most likely lived until about age 50, had dark brown hair, lived in the 1st century, and was not originally from this region of France. There is no scientific way to determine if the skull is Mary's, but the fact that it has been venerated for hundreds of years as if it is seems to create a power of its own. A truth. She existed, this truth insists. She is a real figure of history and not just a legend. This skull has been paraded around Saint-Maximin every July 22 in honor of Mary Magdalene's feast day for hundreds of years.

My eardrum was throbbing from the infection. There was one of those adorable prayer stools right in front of her gold-encased, angel-supported skull. It had red velvet on the cushion for your knees and it creaked a little when I kneeled and placed my elbows on the wooden bar that extends up from the stool so your arms don't get sore before your prayers are completed.

In Mary 9:27, the soul ultimately triumphs. After confronting these seven powers of the ego, the soul is free. "Ignorance has died," the soul tells us. The illusions of the ego that bind the soul are slain. Desires and illusions come to an end. But what's left is what endures, and this is love. This is how I interpret Mary 9:27. Love wins.

As I took a deep breath and began to meditate, all I could hear was this rushing fury of the blood coursing through my heart. My ear infection was creating an earplug effect. The lumbering, clamoring pump of my heart was insanely loud. It was distracting. All I could think about then was how hard it works, always. It's this one constant. Without me even realizing it. It's the one most important sound that keeps me here.

Then in the silence of this inner clamor, I suddenly heard, *"To walk with me is to walk as me."*

Any and all projections were immediately powered down, like a movie projector coming to the end of the film reel. Veneration becomes a very different thing when you're honoring another at eye level. The message to me meant that if Mary Magdalene owned all of her power, she wouldn't want me to give away any of mine.

There can never be a spiritual authority outside of me that is greater than this voice I hear within, this voice of my own uncaged heart.

THE FIFTH POWER

ENSLAVEMENT TO THE PHYSICAL BODY

The Princess of Mercy

For centuries, Quan Yin, the Buddhist deity of compassion, was depicted in iconography as male. But then, at some point in the 7th or 8th century, Quan Yin morphed into a female. And it is believed that "he" became a "she" because of the extraordinary mercy of a princess named Miao Shan.

Miao's dad, the king, was the worst possible man. The kind of man, as his role in the story demands, that it's very difficult to ever want to forgive. He tried to marry off the beautiful and brilliant Miao to an equally horrible, wealthy man three times her age, who lusted after her and wanted her as his prize. And the king wanted to secure more wealth and power for himself through the marriage. So when Miao refused, he banished her to a remote island off the coast of China to live in a monastery.

Miao embraced her banishment. Yes, the island was barren, the nuns were starving, and they were all isolated from the rest of humankind. But, for little Miao, it meant she was free. And all she knew and tasted was the magic of getting to be her radiant, loving self every day.

She didn't see barren earth all around her, but a field of potential. She taught the nuns to garden and plant. And within several years, rumors were beginning to reach the mainland about the succulent vegetables and verdant gardens with beautiful blooms that had turned Miao's island into an actual paradise.

When the king found out that Miao was thriving, that his punishment in a sense had rewarded her, he ordered his guards to travel to the island and burn down the monastery, along with all the food and flowers Miao had helped grow.

Supposedly, just as the monastery caught fire, Miao made it rain, shaman-style, by pricking the tip of her tongue with a hairpin. A torrential rainfall began and quickly put out the raging fire.

This, of course, only made the king more furious. He then sent his executioner to kill Miao Shan for being such a disobedient daughter.

Are you in love with her yet?

I am.

The king's executioner was having a tough time, as he found it difficult to cut off Miao's head. Every form of sword he used, no matter how mighty or sharp, would shatter the instant it touched the skin on Miao's lovely neck. In some versions of her legend, he gives up, and she is spirited away by a glorious, glowing white she-tiger. In other versions, he finally succeeds and, before her last breath, Miao has already forgiven him. And the depth of the mercy he experiences from her forces him to his knees. And so, her executioner becomes her first devotee. Either way, Miao's next stop is hell.

She is spirited away to Yama, ruler of the underworld, and she immediately senses all the people suffering around her. She hears their screams, their urgent cries for help. And because she remains true to who she is, no matter where she is or what anyone has done to her, Miao responds to them with love. And just by turning toward them, listening to them, acknowledging their pain, she witnesses them where they are. This frees them. And so, one by one, Miao liberates each soul and slowly turns hell into heaven.

Freeing souls from hell, however, is bad business for Yama. He knows that unless he wants to oversee an empty realm filled with flowers and souls in full bloom, he needs to kick Miao out. So he sends her back to life, with a gift: the peach of longevity.

She lives in a cave, at this point in her story, as so many female saints seem to love to do at some time in the trajectory of their lives, and she emits an otherworldly fragrance of the most beautiful flowers in bloom. The cave is on the island of Putuo Shan, and she lives here meditating every day for many years, in peace. She becomes well known as a healer, as someone who gives the medicine that only mercy can—an energy that doesn't seek to fix or change, that never judges or shames, but rather just sees, accepts, and remains. A compassion that changes everything just by mirroring back to the one who is suffering that at last their voice has been heard.

News reaches Miao that the king is deathly ill. And that the only way for the king to live is to receive the eyes and the arms of a person who no longer experiences anger. Miao immediately gives her eyes and her arms in order to save the king, her father.

I know.

Really, I seethed, sacrifice?! Martyrdom. This is the last message we could ever need. Self-harm, and self-sacrifice, has nothing to do with true love. I pounded against this story for a while. And I wasn't sure if I wanted to know the ending.

But I had fallen in love with Miao.

So I kept going.

And I remembered, as I forget so easily, that the king is not a man separate from me. I am the king as much as I am Miao. All of these characters, all of the characters of every story, exist within me, within us all.

The king receives her eyes and arms and is restored to health. For the first time in the king's life, he feels grateful. And with that newfound gratitude, he becomes curious about who exactly saved his life. He wanted to meet his savior. He is told that a beautiful hermit living in a remote cave is the reason he's alive. So he travels to her cave to honor her for this profoundly selfless act.

When the king sees that the person who saved his life is Miao, the daughter he had tried to marry off against her will, had banished to be a chaste nun on a desolate island, had attempted to burn out of her home, and had ordered to be executed simply for being the radiant soul that she is—at this, the king falls to his knees at her feet, transfixed by the magnitude of her mercy.

And in that moment, Miao transforms into her true form, the thousand-armed incarnation of compassion, the goddess of mercy, Quan Yin. Flowers of every kind fill her cave, and the radiance of who she truly is can finally be perceived by everyone there to witness her.

This is when I got it.

I suck at math, but I heard her message loud and clear. When I imagined little armless Miao Shan with suddenly a thousand arms, I got the exchange rate. Two arms given with love, not because the recipient deserves those arms, not because the recipient has ever given the giver anything but suffering, but two arms given just for the sake of giving. This level of mercy allows the universe to give back to the giver a thousandfold.

The word *mercy* comes from the Old Etruscan *merc*, meaning "exchange." Cynthia Bourgeault explains that all of life is an exchange because, "'Giving-is-receiving' is the energetic frequency upon which our universe is aligned."[40] We have to give of ourselves, meaning it's when it's hard to give, or when it hurts to give, that we receive the most in the exchange.

And this is because what we lose is the ego. When Miao gives her arms and her eyes to her father, she's symbolically giving away her egoic identity. In handing over her ability to see and her ability to be of physical use in the world, she's detaching herself from her physical body.

She's giving back to him what was actually never hers; his ego's illusion that she was an object at his disposal, that she was a piece of property obligated to obey his desires, that she was a dependent daughter in need of his control to dictate her life, that she was not capable of knowing who she truly is and just how infinitely powerful she has always been.

She gives all these limited beliefs back to him. And then he is able to see out through her eyes and move in the world with the same love that guides her.

Ultimately, the mercy Miao gives the king isn't about him at all. It's about setting her true self free. Whether he deserves her anger or not is irrelevant. If she chooses to remain angry, she chooses to remain chained to him. And this means remaining enslaved to the ego. Forgiving him unbinds her. Forgiving him means she realigns with the law of the universe, which is inherently merciful. The universal law of giving-is-receiving.

Mercy, I think, is the embodiment of compassion. I can have compassion easily for just about anyone. Once I hear how they've suffered, I have compassion on how and why they then perpetuate that suffering by causing harm to others.

What's hard for me is the personal compassion, the mercy that's required of me when I forgive someone who has done me immediate and direct harm. My ego masquerades as this superhero. Hands on her hips. Or like Gandalf, with his staff in the depths of the underworld, proclaiming to that horrible demon-fire-beast, "You shall not pass."

The trouble is that the anger of the ego, even when righteous, can also erect some serious walls in my heart. And this doesn't hurt the person who harmed me; it blocks *me* from the flow of the universe. It disconnects me from what it means to be truly alive, to give and receive love.

Lord Jesus Christ, son of god, have mercy on me.

Mercy is at the heart of the prayer of the heart. Because mercy is what returns us to the heart. Mercy is the power of Christ. A power that isn't a power over, but a power with; mercy is about a perpetual transference of power. Mercy is the energetic exchange at the heart of the universe.

Lord Jesus Christ, son of god, have mercy on me.

The Cave of Eggs

In a world, I was set loose from a world and in a type from a type which is above, and from the chain of forgetfulness which exists in time. From this hour on, for the time of the due season of the aeon, I will receive rest in silence.

— Mary 9:28–29

It was one of those moments when I seriously didn't know what would happen next. I was in yoga gear, because what else do you wear when you're climbing a mountain to visit Mary Magdalene's cave? I was trembling, unsure if I could keep moving forward across the tiny ledge I had somehow managed to climb out on. And I was clutching a small red shoulder bag that had my hotel room key, some Euros in it to pay for the candles I had just lit in her main cave, dark chocolate (I never go anywhere without it), and a map of a place on the mountain I had just found out about the night before—a place I was determined to find called *La Grotte aux Oeufs,* the Cave of Eggs.

Let's back up before I move forward.

I woke up that morning at 5:13. And I screamed at the sight of it. The number 513 was haunting me. I kept waking up at that exact time. And I kept seeing it on receipts, on train tickets. It was everywhere. So, I looked at the little red numbers on the alarm clock and I gave it a wink. I vowed to figure out what that number meant biblically (at some point) and then I rolled over and went back to sleep.

I woke up later, glanced at the alarm, and screamed again when I saw it was already 10 A.M. I had forgotten to set it. The taxi would be picking me up at the convent at 11 A.M. I rinsed off as quickly as I could, put my yoga gear on, and raced downstairs before breakfast ended.

My taxi driver, Veronique, doubles as a tour guide, so she filled me in on much of the local history and belief around Mary Magdalene's arrival in France and her eventual retreat to the cave at Sainte-Baume as we made our way along narrow roads to the base of the mountain.

She said that most believe that Mary Magdalene arrived first in Saintes-Maries-de-la-Mer and preached for many years along the coastal parts of Southern France. Then when the Romans began to persecute the Christians more violently, her brother Lazarus was beheaded. And Saint Maximin wanted her safe. So Mary Magdalene followed a river upstream that runs from the Sainte-Baume mountain down to the Mediterranean.

Veronique told me about the ancient forest that surrounds Mary's cave. She said people travel from all over the world just to see the forest because there are species of trees and plants that exist within it that are unique to this region of France. I was listening to her voice but taking in the stunning landscape of Provence far more until she said, "The Druids considered this forest sacred. It's why they were living in this area before Mary Magdalene arrived. This mountain was sacred long before Christianity claimed it."

Shocked, I pulled for some slack on my seatbelt and turned to face her, "You mean she wasn't here alone?"

Veronique smiled at me, and said, "The church likes to tell the story that Mary Magdalene lived the last 30 years of her life as a hermit in the cave at Sainte-Baume. But that just isn't true. It isn't even possible. She wouldn't have made it one winter alone up there on the mountain. The Druids protected her after her brother Lazarus was killed by the Romans. She fled to this area because they wanted to offer her sanctuary."

It felt odd to be so shocked by something that made so much sense. My picture of her was morphing inside me as the car began its ascent up a steep, winding road. Instead of this almost otherworldly being who basically levitated in meditation, barely ate, and lived in a cave on her own on a mountain in the South of France, I began to see a fully human woman sitting and laughing among others, sharing stories and food around a blazing fire. Of course, she was a part of a community. Of course, a community had supported her.

She was not alone.

I tried to let the reality of that take root in my perception about Mary Magdalene's years spent here on this mountain as I found the path that leads up to her main cave. I walked with intention. Conserving my energy but also beginning to draw my consciousness inward, to the heart.

It takes about an hour to hike up to the main cave. The clearly marked path winds back and forth, getting slightly steeper with each next turn. The slow gradual ascent through thick trees that filtered the light and provided shade from the blazing 100-degree heat let me chant the prayer of the heart with ease. Toward the very end of the trail, at the top of the mountain, there are signs for silence. A few pilgrims passed me and we nodded with smiles and childlike looks of trying not to laugh. There's nothing like forced silence to make you want to bark with laughter.

The higher I climbed the heavier the soundlessness grew. It became a presence I was entering into. A substance thicker than air. I had thought I would cry when I finally reached the entrance to the cave, but I only felt awe, and with each breath inside the cave, I could feel that thick silence spreading throughout my lungs. I was so silent that even my thoughts stopped.

"My dove, in the hidden places of the rocks, in the secret places of the cliffs, show me your form,

and let me hear your voice." — The Song of Songs

La Grotte de Sainte Marie Madeleine first became a pilgrimage site supposedly in 415 A.D. because of the desert father and Hesychast John Cassian after his return from Egypt. Now the Dominican monks maintain it and conduct services every Sunday. Pilgrims can stay in the convent built into the side of the mountain right beside the cave.

I kept expecting the emotions to attack me like some rogue wave. I kept expecting to feel chills, or get feverish. Something.

But all that came to me was this deep reverence in the form of silence. It was a silence that stilled everything.

That's what it was; I was still. Maybe for the first time. Ever. I wasn't thinking, searching, wondering, questioning, fearing, longing, I was just there. Fully. I was spacious and silent inside.

"In a world, I was set loose from a world" sounds like the start of the best movie trailer ever made. What Mary 9:28 is articulating is that while Mary was in the world, she was set free from it. Meaning, she didn't have to wait to die to be cut loose from the egoic binds that tied her here.

"World" here, it's important to explain, is the world that we each perceive. It's personal. It's not world as in our shared planet. It's world as in our individual realities. And yet we all have this same template of seven powers of the ego that impose suffering on us in varying measure. And we all have this same potential, to be set free from this "world," while we're still very much in it.

"In a type from a type which is above" is reminding us of what ultimately frees us; the nous, the highest aspect of the soul that we can perceive while here, embodied. We remember that we are not just this ego, this mass of seemingly endless desires the ego creates, but we are a soul; we are *"from a type which is above."*

Remembering this is the antidote. Remembering that we are essentially good, essentially this nous at the heart of each of our own worlds is what breaks the "chain of forgetfulness." Remembering that the body exists in time, but the soul does not. The soul is not of this "world." This is what can free us, even if for some of us, only for a moment.

I went to the back of the cave behind the small wooden pews and behind the main altar. A friend had told me about the Mary Magdalene statue there and all the love notes pilgrims leave at her feet. It's a statue of Mary in ecstasy. Her head is thrown back, her eyes are closed. She's clearly receiving something from within her. I had brought my red pen and a few torn pages from my journal. I wrote prayers for loved ones, folded each up, and tossed them among the sea of others.

In Mary 9:29, *"I will receive rest in silence,"* I can feel the way the war within Mary has come to an end. The rest is the bliss that comes after the demons, the powers, those loud egoic voices have been overcome. The "rest" comes because she knows herself completely. She knows that this "silence" within her heart is the treasure; this is where she can rest in love.

"Silence" to me means the calm quiet that comes when fear has lost its voice. Silence here, again, is not an absence of sound, it's the end of the clamor, the racket the ego makes. It's the rest we can receive when all we are hearing is the sound of what the heart contains.

I lit seven tall taper candles on an altar against the far wall of the cave. Then I wrapped the red shawl I had fortunately brought with me tightly around my shoulders and sat down to take in the light the candles emitted. I turned from the candles and the dark cold wall of the cave and stared at the light streaming in through the stained-glass windows. One is of a long-dark-haired Mary Magdalene sitting at a white round table being served a feast with Christ. Another one is of Mary Magdalene pouring water over Christ's head.

She was not alone. And he was not alone.

The stillness lifted. Just like that. I was suddenly restless to find the Cave of Eggs. And if it was as difficult as Rose suggested, then I only had a handful of hours before it got too dark to find it. So, I set out, without water, or any sense of what direction I should be heading.

The only people I had passed on the trails for the past hour were in full-on hiking gear with water bottles and those strange hats that have flaps that cover the back of the neck. I wasn't sure what made their expressions of confusion more pronounced, the fact that I was out on the mountain dressed like a lost tourist or that I was asking them in my heavily American-accented French if they knew where I could find La Grotte aux Oeufs. No one seemed to understand what I was saying, or when they did, they didn't know where the cave might be. But I refused to give up.

And this is how I found myself several hours later, panting in the heat, clinging to the side of a trail no wider than my two feet and trembling at the reality that I could fall. Far. Sweat was beading across my forehead. There was zero shade. The fierce sun in the cerulean sky reminded me how exposed and unprepared I was to set off and find this mysterious place on my own.

There I was out on a ledge like a stranded baby goat thinking about the possible titles to the newspaper article reporting my disappearance. And realizing that only Rose even knew I'd gone to find the Cave of Eggs that day. In my rush that morning, I hadn't told anyone back home.

I couldn't move forward, and I couldn't move backward.

This is when I met my savior. I could hear her long before I could see her. She was whistling. It made me think of the legend of Brigid, the Celtic goddess who supposedly invented whistling so people walking through the dark can call out to each other and know they're not alone.

She made the most compassionate coo-ing noises when she saw me on the trail. She knew two things instantly, no doubt: first, that I was American and second that I was evidently completely lost. The thing is, she couldn't get past me and I couldn't move. I was too terrified to keep inching my way forward across the ledge. She was followed by a teenage boy, two teenaged girls, and a man with a cigarette dangling from his mouth. Very slowly and carefully, she figured out a way to step past me. (I had pretty much pressed myself flat against the side of the mountain.) Then she reached out her hand from behind her and made this odd, "Alle, alle, alle ooop" rally cry that we just don't have in English. But it felt so reassuring.

I just couldn't picture plummeting to my death to such a crazy and strangely comforting sound. I was not going to die with "Alle, alle, alle ooop" as the last thing I ever heard. I held tightly to her hand and shuffled sideways across the ledge with my face still pressed to the mountain. She stopped as soon as we made it to a wider clearing. My heart was flamenco dancing in my chest.

The rest of the group circled up and opened their backpacks to drink water. She offered me a sip from her water bottle, I was so clearly out of breath. And I gave her my last chunk of dark chocolate. We smiled, wordlessly agreeing on the equity of those two essentials.

In French, I have the vocabulary of a three-year-old. So I told them in my toddler French that I was writing a book about Mary Magdalene and wanted to find the Cave of Eggs. Alle Ooop's eyes immediately lit up with recognition and she shot her fists triumphantly into the air, LA GROTTE AUX OEUFS!!! Miraculously, we were all looking for the same place. So, we set off together, emboldened by our chance meeting and common destination.

After another hour of hiking, and after passing several sets of pilgrims who couldn't point us in the right direction, we stopped by a boulder with a small *cairn*, or rock pile, that pilgrims leave for Mary Magdalene to bless them with fertility.

Alle Ooop passed me her water bottle again. The kids were getting tired and wanted to return to the café that was at the base of the mountain. We looked at each other and realized that we might not make it to the cave. It suddenly hit me then that I hadn't prayed. I suggested to her that we ask Mary Magdalene for guidance. So Alle Ooop and I closed our eyes and said a prayer together for the way to be revealed.

As soon as we got back on the trail, two hikers came into view, clearly pros, decked out with those metal sticks that look like ski poles for managing down the steep terrain. Alle Ooop and I took one look at each other and knew this was our last chance. Her sudden expression of excitement is sealed in my heart for good. Her eyebrows were clear up to her hairline.

She asked them in rapid-fire French as they passed if they knew how to find the Cave of Eggs. And when they responded with an enthusiastic yes, our little band of exhausted pilgrims erupted into delirious hoots of all kinds and ecstatic high-fives. And then we all shot our hands into the air like Alle Ooop and yelled, "La Grotte aux Oeufs!"

We hiked for maybe just 20 more minutes, made our way through some green shrubs that obscured our view, and then there it was. The Cave of Eggs. The yoni of the mountain.

My little family of pilgrims all whipped out headlamps from their backpacks and put them on. I marveled at the grace I felt in having met up with them. Without them I wouldn't have made it here. We were meant to find the cave together.

I helped one of the teenage girls down the slippery slope that led into the cave. There were chilling and bizarre egg-shaped indentations in the side of the cave wall that I wouldn't have been able to see without the light that they brought down into the dark. I was mesmerized.

The teen I had helped down started to get claustrophobic. Alle Ooop took off her headlamp (without saying a word) and handed it to me so I could stay in the cave alone while she led the kids back up.

I could hear the echo of water trickling even deeper down into the cave. There was an endless sound to it and a timeless feel to the place where I was standing. It was cold enough to see my breath. The walls of the cave were glistening wet. I tried to take in what I was seeing.

This was the place I had wanted to find for most of my life. A place where the memory of Mary Magdalene isn't once removed. A place where my life could overlap with hers. A place where I felt as though I was encountering not her words, or her legend, not her teachings, or the stories that have been told about her, but the actual human woman.

I felt elated to sense her humanity, to have stood where I felt certain she had been.

I thought of salvation then. The definition of it as something that comes from within, salvation as simply "to be made more alive." Because this is what happened to me in the Cave of Eggs. I was made more alive. What was within me was here, met from the outside. It wasn't happiness. That's too fleeting. I stared at the eggs, at the gorgeous, miraculous-looking ovals in the cave wall, and I felt radiant. Luminous. Nothing, and no one, ever, can take from me what I encountered right then. This is the thing itself, and not a prayer, or a song, or a story. This is the love that sits hidden within us. This is the love that never ends.

I felt that other side of myself, the side I met with that last time I saw the shaman, and when I first saw the red thread. The side I thought I would always find in someone else. In romantic love. And for all these years, for all my broken hearts, I have resented and resisted this truth: that this love I've always known and desired is right here within me. It's the other half of who I am.

And this is what it means to rest in silence. Because this is when all those voices, those ideas and stories we wrestle with inside us, the ones that keep us up at night, and lead us to believe we aren't worthy of love, or of anything good, this is when the whole clamorous riot goes mute.

This is when we understand what freedom is. The silence that returns us to love.

When we all were gathered around a large table at the café at the base of the mountain, drinking ice cold Schweppes, the man in our little band of pilgrims turned to speak to me for the first time and asked in his thick French accent, "What does Mary Magdalene mean for you?"

I took a while to answer. And then I asked him the same question. He just lifted his hand and placed it on his chest and said, "Isis and Mary Magdalene are the same here in my heart." I stared at him, a frank look of pure shock on my face. It's always the quiet ones.

When I checked out of Le Couvent Royale, the total was 520 euros for the week I was there. I had a moment of anticipation that it would total 513, the number that had been harassing me since I arrived in France. As the receptionist went over the bill, I Googled Druids and saw that they were Celtic priests and priestesses from a tradition that existed long before Christianity.

Then just because I wanted the haunting of 5:13 to end, I made good on my vow from early that morning and Googled what scripture it refers to. When I read Galatians 5:13, I got chills. And I knew it was the message meant for me: *"Brothers and sisters, you are called here to be free."*

This is when the receptionist let me know she had accidentally charged me for a room tax with two occupants rather than just me alone. She reconfigured the total. Yep, 513.

She Who Confirms the Truth

After Mary had said these things, she was silent. Since it was up to this point that the Savior had spoken to her.

— Mary 9:30–31

Le Sacré-Coeur, the Sacred Heart cathedral, is high on a hill in Montmartre, in Paris. Walking up the winding path, even when it's packed with tourists, is magical to me. My favorite Christ is up there. He's made of a gold mosaic in a dome that arches over the main altar. His arms are outstretched and he's radiating this form of embrace that blows my composure every time.

Donna, author of *Sex and the Soul* and the friend I had in common with the man seated at my table on the *Queen Mary,* met me in Paris for several days. She's a walker, like me. Our little hotel was near the Eiffel Tower, so we decided to walk all the way from the 7th arrondissement of Paris across the Seine to the 18th arrondissement, where the Sacred Heart cathedral is located.

When we finally arrived, Donna groaned at the crowds. There was a line wrapping around the cathedral with a security checkpoint stationed in front of the gate. Everyone was frisked to get inside. I talked Donna into waiting. I built up the anticipation. And like a child in line at an amusement park, I fluttered with sheer excitement.

We were ushered around to the left, partitioned off from the main pews in the center of the cathedral for those who came to pray, not just snap photos and beeline it for the gift shop. The outer circle for tourists moved slowly past small altars dedicated to various saints.

When we got to the enclave for Mother Mary, Donna wanted to stop. She paid for a small votive, lit it, and let this soft light suddenly shine from her face. I knew she was saying a prayer for her mother who had passed of cancer years ago. Her mother had loved Mary. *Devoted*. That's the word Donna used, her mother was devoted to Mary.

This particular statue of Mother Mary is exceptionally beautiful. She's in a glass-enclosed altar. Her arms are outstretched with her open palms facing upward. She has a golden sacred heart in the center of her chest. There's a little gate at the entrance to her separate little enclave within the cathedral. I opened it so I could get a closer look at her. A little girl, no more than three, was holding the gate shut when I turned around to leave. Her mother was laughing and repeating to her in French, "Rose, open the door."

I kneeled down to Rose's height, so we could be eye to eye, and I smiled into her cherub face. "I get it, little one. You want me to stay here and pray to Mary."

The polarity of Mother Mary the virgin and Mary Magdalene the prostitute has always seemed a bit too familiar, too contrived to be true. Jean-Yves Leloup, in *The Sacred Embrace of Jesus and Mary*, explains, "We have forgotten to represent the other side of Christ, his feminine side, in a way beyond the reductionist stereotypes of mother and whore."[41]

Like Mary Magdalene, Mary of Nazareth, Christ's mother, was said to have always walked with him. And she was there throughout his ministry and there with Mary Magdalene at the foot of the cross at his crucifixion. She was also there, according to some legends, with Mary Magdalene on the ship without sails that arrived in the South of France in the 1st century. There's a legend that relates she returned to or never left Jerusalem, where she was assumed by the angels into heaven at the moment of her death.

Mary, Christ's mother, has been represented as the virgin, just as Mary Magdalene has been represented as the whore, based on ideas of the church that didn't form until centuries after Christ's crucifixion. In 431 A.D., at the council of Ephesus, Mary was declared *Theotokos*, god-bearer, or more simply put, the Mother of God. She was, therefore, subsequently declared as immaculate, the

Ever-Virgin. Some other titles she has been given over the years include the Queen of Heaven, Our Lady of the Angels, Our Lady of Good Council, Our Lady Undoer of Knots, and She Who Confirms the Truth.

She was born without the "sin" that the church fathers had established by the 4th century that sex and procreation entailed. This idea of sin did not exist before then. (And it does not exist in the Gospel of Mary.) This is important to not forget; women weren't present during the council of Ephesus, so women did not get to help create the story that would shape the birth of institutionalized Christianity.

I'm ready for a Mary that is a third option, a middle between these extremes that touches to the truth more faithfully. A Mary who isn't a whore or a virgin. Or, a Mary that is both, like the voice in *The Thunder, Perfect Mind*: "I am the whore, and the holy woman. I am the wife and the virgin." I turned back to Mary's statue, to her outstretched arms and her open palms.

I stared at her golden heart. And I imagined that moment in Christian belief when the angel Gabriel announced to her that she would give birth to god.

What's so profound about Mary is that the "yes" she said to that surge of light that came in the form of an angel within her, a yes that she never uttered outside of her, became one of the greatest expansions of love in the history of religions.

I nodded in humility to Mary. To her courageousness that's still left so unacknowledged, and uncelebrated. She should be riding a tiger like the Hindu goddess Durga. We don't get yet how powerful it is to be that wide open to the voice of love, to be that present to the light inside the heart. And then to make our life about that union.

Donna ushered me on. We made our way past the rest of the semicircle of altars that line the inside of the cathedral, then entered the tourist-free, roped-off area for the real prayers. She led us to a pew that was virtually empty and right beneath the golden Christ I had returned to the Sacred Heart cathedral to see. The second we sat down, this thick, sweet, honey-like silence spilled over me. I couldn't move. And I couldn't hear anything except that tumultuous, expectant silence inside me.

I looked up and took Christ in from this proximity. I noticed that there's a little Joan of Arc kneeling at his feet. She's suited up in full armor, down on one knee. Her sword is gold and off to one side. How could I have missed her? Joan of Arc, and her hauntingly brave mantra before entering the Hundred Years' War in France as a teenaged soldier, "I am not afraid, I was born to do this." She, like Mary, had said yes to the angel she heard within her.

I asked a question then, in my heart. I had been feeling, sensing, half-believing I wouldn't come back from this pilgrimage. Or, said another way, I knew I would not come back the same.

I asked if I would see my son again.

I thought about Mary as I asked this. The love of her son. Being with a soul from the moment of conception, to first breath, to first steps, and first words, and first love. And then last steps, and last words, and last breath. It's such an uncelebrated vocation, to love a boy to manhood, to completion. To raise a man who has been initiated by the feminine.

Marion Woodman in *Conscious Femininity* relates that when we as a culture can raise the divine masculine from infancy to manhood, we will have moved the Christian story forward. We will have witnessed the rise of the divine masculine, a masculinity that can only come through a merging of the masculine with the feminine.

Christ in this form, at the Sacred Heart, fully clothed in robes of gold and light, crowned with a halo that reaches in the four directions, and with arms as wide as the ceiling of the cathedral, is the masculine I love. Integrated. Whole. Feeling. Embracing. And most importantly, enduring.

Then, I heard and felt the sweet exhale of the answer, *yes*.

I know I will see my son again. I trust this. Even as everything is uncertain. I will see him again.

And then something more happened. I feel the awareness of what love really does. I feel the way love functions as a bridge. That in loving we can't ever be separate from those we love. *Cor ad cor loquitur,* which is Latin for "heart speaks to heart directly." I am only ever as far away from him as I allow myself to believe I am. I am only as far from him as I am from my own heart.

I miss him. And instead of thinking this, I tell this to him directly. I remember that I am with him always, from within. I tell him how much I miss him and just how much I love him.

I look up at this Christ, this embodiment of enduring love set in gold, with arms that take in the whole mass of us, sitting there in the pews, silently praying, silently saying everything we need to say into our hearts. We think our hearts are separate and our own. But really, the heart is like a walkie-talkie, if we know how to use it. And when we have the courage to get still enough to go inward, it's like we're pressing down on that little red plastic bit on the side and speaking directly into a receiver.

Then when we release our grip on that little red plastic bit that lets us speak to the soul, to god, to spirit—however you experience it or whoever you think is holding the matching walkie-talkie—you lift up on the button and wait, expectantly, in silence. Until suddenly, there's a crackling noise and then a stream of light from a voice within you.

Mary 9:30–31, *"After Mary had said these things, she was silent. Since it was up to this point that the Savior had spoken to her,"* reminds us that everything we've been hearing since Mary 6, when Peter asks Mary to teach them about what has been hidden from them, is a conversation that took place *within* Mary. It makes certain to remind us that these secret teachings came to her, that Christ revealed to her alone, because she could hear him, from *within* her.

Mary and Christ had walkie-talkie hearts.

And what I could feel in that moment beneath his wide embrace is that I do too. We all do.

If we know how to use them.

The next day at breakfast, Donna and I were planning our visit to the Chapel of Our Lady of the Miraculous Medal on Rue du Bac. As I waited for my omelet to arrive, I checked my email and saw that Lisbeth, the artist for *The Divine Feminine Oracle*, had uploaded her first draft of the card for Saint Catherine Labouré. My jaw dropped at the timing. She's the saint who had the vision of the Virgin Mary at the exact chapel I was about to see for the first time that morning.

Catherine saw a vision of Mary, similar to the stance Mary's statue is in at the Sacred Heart cathedral, with her arms outstretched and her palms open. Except in Catherine's vision, rays of light were streaming out of Mary's palms. She said that the light was the healing, the answered prayers rushing from her to everyone who calls out to her.

Catherine also asked Mary a question in her vision. She noticed that there were rays that weren't reaching our world. They were sort of ricocheting off the world's surface and going into space. Catherine asked Mary what that was all about. And Mary said, "Those are the graces for which people forget to ask."

Spirit is so mindful, so ethical, that we have to ask on behalf of ourselves and others to be blessed with healing. We have to love ourselves enough to ask for assistance.

Donna did the same face-morphing thing that she'd done at Sacred Heart when she lit a candle for her mom. Her features just sort of transformed from normal-looking human skin to glowing particles of light. She's so unassumingly Catholic. So unceremoniously spiritual. No rosary. No mention really ever of Christ or Mary. But get her in a cathedral and she'll transubstantiate right in front of you.

Donna then made her way to a seat in the pews, but I wanted to do some close-up praying right beneath the statue of Mary that's lit with a golden halo at the center of the altar in the cathedral. A woman beside me, from Senegal I later learned, had tears streaming down both cheeks. I heard her pray in a language I didn't comprehend but my heart understood. *Cor ad cor loquitur.* I went to pray for myself, but when I heard her suffering, I started immediately praying for her. And I instantly felt lighter. And this is what is so paradoxical. (As the truth, apparently, inherently is.) When I empty myself, when I forget myself for the sake of someone else, I'm instantly filled beyond what I could have ever asked for myself.

Maybe this is what grace needs; the moment when the sudden love we have for a perfect stranger eclipses what we think we know, what we think we need, and just takes over. Maybe this is what Mary did in that moment when Gabriel asked her if she would give birth to god. Would she eclipse herself, and her own little life, the story she was living with Joseph, the future they were beginning to script for themselves? Would she let spirit write her story instead? Could she say yes to this light inside her?

THE SIXTH POWER

THE FALSE PEACE OF THE FLESH

The Whole Point Is That It Never Ends

Even if it only comes and goes. Even if you hide it from others. Especially if you hide it from yourself. Even if it scares you. Especially if it scares you.

Even if you wonder some days if it was ever real. Even if you think deep down that it's someone else's. Even if you think its beauty has nothing to do with you.

Even if you haven't seen it in so long it feels lost to you. Especially if it feels lost to you. Even if it's buried so deep you have to mine past the hardest parts of you.

Even if it's only your secret. Especially if it's only your secret. Even if it's just a grain of sand. A mustard seed. I want you to know that your love is enough.

You can always begin again.

I have this deeply held belief that there's this place I'll reach, this state of mind—meaning heart—where I become too aware, too conscious, to be hurt again or too enlightened to fall down neck deep in the mess of my ego. I keep thinking there will be this "X marks the spot," this plateau where I arrive, this place where I free myself once and for all from myself.

But there is no there.

The whole point is that it never ends.

It isn't a failure to feel human, to be broken by heartbreak. It's the whole point. The choice we have, the opportunity that's presented to us in those moments of exquisite pain, is to also remember the soul. We can bring in the other half of what it means to be human. Not right away, or at least not at first. We can just let it sit on our shoulder or in our back pocket. And even that little presence of light might help us move through the pain differently than we had before.

We might be able to see new responses to a pain that is as ancient as scripture.

Try not to curse the pain, or avoid it. Or to feel like a failure because of it. Try not to run from it, and numb it. Try to see it as our chance to reach a love that can withstand it. Not permanently; nothing is permanent. Just in this moment. That's all that matters. Find the presence of love in those moments when before you had abandoned yourself. Even if it's just a little love, a grain of sand, a mustard seed.

Your love is enough.

Love Has Already Won

After examining these matters, Peter said, "Has the Savior spoken secretly to a woman and not openly so that we would all hear? Surely, he did not want to show that she is more worthy than we are?" Then Mary wept and said to Peter, "My brother Peter, what are you imagining? Do you think that I have thought up these things by myself in my heart or that I am telling lies about the Savior?"

— **MARY 10:3–6**

There was a bird in the rafters above us. The ladies at Dartington Hall in Devon had tried to get the little creature out before the workshop began. But it seemed he wanted to stay. It was a sparrow, which is common to that area in the southwest of England. I loved its unexpected dashes from one rafter to the next, filling the air with the clamor of its furious wings.

If I was Dorothy in the *Wizard of Oz*, and I clicked my ruby-red slippers, home would always be here. Not here in Devon necessarily, but here, in a circle of women. We were in more of an oval, actually, so that we could all fit in the rectangular barn-like space I was invited to teach in that day. And as I looked at every face in the circle, I felt this galactic exhale. As I always do.

When I sit in a circle, I know my body will communicate more than anything I end up saying.

It says, wordlessly, just by being at eye level with everyone else:

There is no hierarchy to the spiritual world. We are all equal. And we're all equally trying, in our own crazy ways, to love ourselves enough to see the good that's right here with us.

For me, what I have witnessed in a circle of women for the past two decades is captured perfectly in Mary 10:3. We have the issue of worth that runs deep, 2,000 years deep. And we have the issue that as women we won't be believed when we tell the truth. I see again and again this systemic problem with knowing that we are worthy of having a voice, and believing in it.

First, let's talk about Peter.

After Peter is the one to ask Mary (in Mary 6:1–2) to tell them, the other disciples, what the savior revealed to her that is still hidden from them (because the savior loved her more than all other women), and after Mary very lovingly (in Mary 7–9) reveals to them everything she was taught (because of her love for Christ) Peter doesn't believe her.

(And neither does Andrew, in Mary 10:1. He says he doesn't believe her because Mary's teachings are "strange." Personally, I read "strange" as a compliment. Anyway, we're focusing on Peter. But just so you realize, Peter wasn't alone in his disbelief.)

He says, *"Has the savior spoken secretly to a woman and not openly so that we would all hear? Surely, he did not want to show that she is more worthy than we are?"* The two words in Peter's reaction that stand out to me as if they're on fire are the words "woman" and "worth."

WOMAN: He can't believe that Christ could possibly reveal to Mary what he didn't reveal to them. How could she, Mary, a woman (the lesser sex), be more deserving?

WORTH: He can't believe that as a woman she could be worthy of such secret teachings. The worth he's questioning here is that of the female, and also of the feminine. How could she hear him from within her? How could she be worthy of such an intimate proximity to Christ?

And then Mary weeps.

Hurt, she asks Peter, *"Do you think that I have thought up these things by myself in my heart or that I am telling lies about the Savior?"*

She weeps, yes, because she isn't believed. She's betrayed after trusting them with her secret teachings, with the things she knows by heart. But I think she weeps also because she was given a transmission that she realizes now the disciples are not able to receive. It's a teaching that she can uniquely give to them precisely because their whole world order and idea of power would have to shift in order to receive it.

I think it's easy to identify with Mary. The one who in the 1st century, according to the Roman hierarchy of power, would be considered the least powerful among them. The one Peter sees as the least deserving. The one who, after sharing her heart with those she thought were friends, family even, is betrayed. The one who isn't believed. And who, after being called a liar, is then lied about for 2,000 years.

And maybe it's easy to identify with Peter also. Maybe we are all Peter at those times in our lives when we question how we could possibly deserve a love that's right here, within us.

And maybe what made Mary worthy of such a love was that she knew worth had nothing to do with it. Maybe Mary was more loved by Christ than any other because she knew that she wasn't separate from his love in the first place.

If we are caught up in trying to prove or earn or show that we're worthy of love, we're missing out on the actual presence of it. In the Gospel of Thomas, Christ says, "If you bring forth what is within you, what is within you will save you."

I think this is what was hidden that Mary revealed: that love is within us. We are love, and we don't have to earn or prove or deserve this fact. And if we can recognize that we've never been separate from it, and bring it forth outside of us, this is what saves us.

Or at least for a moment, and then we go back to being Peter and questioning what we deserve. And this is what it is to be human. To walk around with this heaven, this treasure of love, here in the heart. And to do this crazy dance of trying to feel worthy of it.

I suggested to the ladies in Devon that what Mary Magdalene represents in her gospel is the *anthropos*, the child of true humanity, the true human being, meaning, the person who has remembered she is fully human and fully divine. She is a flaming ego, and an eternal soul of love. The fact that she could perceive Christ from within her proves that she had merged with the angel within her, the nous, the soul. She was what we can be also.

I think the deepest wounds hold the most powerful medicine. I think the reason I feel transformed every time I sit in a circle of women and just listen to each other try, and falter, and try again to love ourselves enough to tell the truth is because it reaches back to Mary Magdalene. It helps correct an ancient wrong by believing myself and other women. It helps heal this imbalance of power by participating in a power that's shared, that comes from within.

I asked us to close our eyes. I had this little punk renegade fearful thought that kept riding past my more serene thoughts, like Ron Perlman on his Harley-Davidson in *Sons of Anarchy*. It was my fear of having to fly back to the States. I led us then in a soul-voice meditation.

I suggested that we imagine a golden light like a full body halo surrounding us. Fierce light. As if it's tearing through the fabric of reality as it carves out space for us to just hear ourselves. I suggested that this golden light, like the porousness of an eggshell, lets us release right now in this moment anything that's no longer serving us. (Ron Perlman rode straight out through the light.) And it also allows in any guidance or support that we might need in this moment.

Then I asked for us to take that first intentional breath, the breath that would drop us like an anchor into the heart. In this circle of women, in Devon, that first breath was like jumping on a Slip 'N Slide. I'm not sure if I've ever reached my heart as quickly.

I asked us then to take the second intentional breath. And know that we can become aware of the soul this easily. Anything we ask in the heart is answered. Everything we seek inwardly, we find.

I suggested we ask then, from within the heart, "What do I need to know in this moment?"

I exhaled and sat there in the circle like a cat on the edge of a couch in the sun. I never wanted to move.

I heard the answer then, of what I needed to know in this moment, *love has already won.*

Love has already won.

After sitting in silence for some time, I asked us to give gratitude as we take our third breath together. And that when we open our eyes, we are now seeing with the eye of the heart.

I looked around the room and blasted each woman with a fire hose full of light. My beloved REDLADY Ger was among them. These unassuming warriors have all just fought a battle that's unseen. It's the very real struggle to hear the voice of love inside them. And to believe it. To believe it enough that they can act now on its directives.

All I want to give them is this memory Mary's teachings have given me: *Love has already won.* When we forget, when we give up on ourselves, tomorrow or next week, or when we slowly start to feel that heavy mantle of shame that isn't ours to wear, and we allow ourselves to be treated in harmful ways, or we don't rage against those who treat us harmfully, I want us to have this memory of what it feels like to be held. To just be in a love that has been here all along.

In about three days, I'll be clutching the flight attendant's hand during takeoff. I will have utterly forgotten everything I knew in that circle in Devon. The power of craving will have me completely blind to all else; I will crave desperately not to die. I will be visibly trembling. Concerned, the flight attendant will have moved us to the back of the plane so we can sit together in two empty seats. She will stare into my eyes until I am back behind them again. And I'll tear up not because I'm afraid—which I am, I'm petrified—but because I get (again) that the whole point is that it never ends. We keep remembering and forgetting. We keep merging with that presence and then separating. We are here for each other. We need each other to remember that, as tough and terrifying as it gets, love has already won. Love is this merciful transference of power. Love is this compulsion to help, and this humility to be helped.

The metaphysical text *A Course in Miracles* says, "The holiest place on earth is where an ancient hatred has become a present love." This is what it feels like for me every time I can let love be present here in this body that has known trauma and pain. This fragile, fleeting body becomes the holiest place on earth.

The sparrow, I later found out, is said to have been the only bird present during Christ's crucifixion. It became symbolic of the triumph that comes after a long time of suffering.

The White Spring

Levi said to Peter, "Peter, you are always ready to give way to your perpetual inclination to anger. And even now you are doing exactly that by questioning the woman as though you're her adversary."

— **Mary 10:7–8**

I had returned to Glastonbury to lead a soul-voice meditation for another circle of women on a retreat at the Chalice Well led by a friend, Rebecca, author of *Rise Sister Rise.* And I was there to return to Glastonbury with my love, Kyle, author of *Light Warrior.* The first night, Kyle and I went on a spiritual double date with our friend Lisa, author of *Witch: Unleashed. Untamed. Unapologetic,* and her husband, Rich, who has the best bear hug in the entire world. And our date included an unexpected skinny-dip into the cistern of the White Spring.

I had no intention of stripping naked. But there's something about that primal space that compelled me to. There was very little volition involved. Maybe none. Sweet Rich averted his eyes, Kyle rolled them, and Lisa locked hers with mine in that way that only ladies who love each other through everything can.

And I wasn't really naked. Or I didn't *feel* naked at all, even though I very quickly didn't have any clothing on. It felt as if with each next thing I took off, my jeans, my bra, I was joining something. I was entering a different reality. I was getting closer to an understanding of why I had been so drawn to be there, to the Red and White springs. I was becoming more fully clothed in something that can't be seen with the eye.

I wasn't cold. I should have been. The others were exhaling little wisps of smoke that their breath made visible by the chill in the air. I knew it was cold, but I experienced the freezing water as an intensity rather than a temperature; the cold was a searing clarity. I didn't resist it, so there wasn't any pain as I walked to the center of the cistern, naked, and cloaked in the memory of who I have always been.

What I felt was a pride that went deep into my bones. No, it was a pride that came from within them, through them. A pride that could never be extracted. It was a pride in me, in the woman I am that coursed through my body, my blood, my veins as if through all the centuries, as if it had always existed.

Lisa was singing a song that felt hauntingly familiar to me. It filled the crypt of the White Spring with its timeless beauty. My eyes filled with tears.

The song seemed to be asking me, "*What do I know that I don't need anyone else to know with me? What is true because I can feel that it is, not because it's in scripture or ordained as true?*"

The Petrine Doctrine is the belief that Saint Peter was given special authority by Christ that has since passed on to each Pope. It's an entirely male succession of power and spiritual authority. It's the outcome of this dispute that's so evident in Mary's gospel. Peter does not believe her. He does not believe that she was given secret teachings from Christ to pass on to the other disciples.

So, although Levi comes to Mary's defense in Mary 10:7–8, and although he represents a voice of the early Christ movement that believed Mary, we know that ultimately her gospel will be destroyed (and buried—kiss those Copts) within the next 300 years, and that by 594, in Pope Gregory's homily 33, her story will be retold, branding her as the prostitute.

Mary's status as the companion of Christ, the first to receive his teachings on how to perceive him from within the heart and how to become unified ourselves, will all be lost for millennia.

Jesus says in the Gospel of Thomas, "When you strip off your clothes without being ashamed, and you take your clothes and put them under your feet like children and trample them, then you will see the living one and you will not be afraid."[42] And in the

Gospel of Philip, Jesus relates, "They who make themselves simple, to the point of nakedness, are not naked."[43]

What we wear without realizing it is the ego. It's the stories we've covered ourselves with, or the stories we have used to obscure the truth of who we really are. And the ego is so well meaning. It's like this helicopter mom who thinks we need protection and thinks fear will keep us safe. The ego builds up all these layers of why we should be afraid of who we are, or why we should feel shame about who we have been.

And the power that is the most crippling, or blinding, is the last power, the seventh (even though as you've recognized within you, there isn't a consecutive order to the powers). It's the one Levi says that Peter has been overcome by in Mary 10:7, *"Peter, you are always ready to give way to your perpetual inclination to anger."* After Mary reveals the secret teachings that Christ gave her, and her alone, I can imagine Peter was angry. He became a saint but he was also human. And I can imagine he might have felt betrayed, since he didn't receive these secret teachings as well. He's angry, and in his anger, he treats Mary as if she is an adversary and not his sister.

His anger, a power of the ego, and the anger of those who followed him, changed the course of Christianity to exclude Mary, to shift her from the one Christ loved completely and steadfastly to the one Christ healed of seven "demons." Peter, and those Peter represents, didn't seem to get the parables Christ used to suggest to us that we "get naked" so we can see each other with a clarity of heart the ego obscures.

As you know now, the ego has seven incarnations, attributes, or powers, according to the Gospel of Mary. These are the "demons" that supposedly Christ drew from Mary. And the answer of what to do to free ourselves of these powers could not be easier. Just get naked. Every time the ego tries to dress you again in an old story of what you're capable of, or of the victim you once were, or of what you need to be afraid of, or of why you need to remain small, just take it off. Strip. Skinny-dip. Repeat.

(I'm speaking metaphorically here. But, of course, if actually getting naked helps, more power to you.)

Cynthia Bourgeault believes that Christ's process of freeing himself and becoming *ihidaya,* becoming the "unified one," had everything to do with mastering the art of kenosis. Kenosis comes from the Greek verb *kenosein,* which means "to empty oneself." She believes that Christ is able to endure and ultimately overcome "Satan" because he never takes the bait that keeps getting dangled for his ego to latch on to.

He remains still; he rests in emptiness. Bourgeault explains, "Stripping oneself and standing naked: this is the essence of the kenotic path."[44]

According to conventional wisdom, 40 days is what it takes to break an addictive thought pattern. The thought pattern in turn causes addictive behaviors and actions. And these behaviors and actions can become habituated, unconscious even.

I've always loved that Christ was in the wilderness (of his own mind) for 40 days being tested by "Satan" (the ego he needed to meet with inside him). And that really, this is not something that was done once and then done with forever. This was a powerful spiritual tool that he used to integrate his soul with his body, his mind with his heart. This is how he was able to unify the angel within him to his physical form. Getting naked. Again and again.

When a past love reveals the reason why they left, when a parent lets you know what more you could do to find success, when a beloved friend betrays you, when you hear a voice within you telling you you're not enough, you're not worthy, you won't ever be truly loved—this is what I took off when I stood in the cistern of the White Spring.

And this is when I felt a pride that went all the way back and all the way through. A pride in being human. In struggling, and failing, and in sometimes reaching this state of exalted light.

THE SEVENTH POWER

THE COMPULSION OF RAGE

What We Have Remembered

Where does the rage originate?

First it was when your best friend left. The one who remembered you. The one you fell in love with. The one you trusted more than yourself. The one who made sure any pain and suffering you went through soon had meaning.

Then it was your husband. Your partner. Your son's father. The one who changed his mind, who hardened his heart after you had already handed yours to him. To hold, to harbor like a sparrow in his palm.

First it was your best friend and then your husband.

No, this isn't where it began.

First, it was the teenager who crept into his sister's room while you slept, while you were in the last trusting sleep you would ever have, the one who confused you for an object, the one who had no idea that what he was doing severed you from your body.

Then there was your best friend, and then there was your husband.

No, this isn't when it started.

First, there was that moment in Sunday school, when you read how women were silenced, how they were only ever the supporting actresses in this variation of a story about god, and how the presence that you sensed before you went to church had been left out. What was within you was not outside of you, and this was the beginning.

No, the first betrayal is every time you remain silent about what you hear in your heart. That is the most primal deception, this inability or unwillingness to trust what you hear inside you, in this voice that doesn't have a voice without you.

And this is understandable. This inability to be a bridge between what you hear in your heart and what you say out loud. Christ says in Mary 3:14, "Anyone with two ears capable of hearing should listen!" We're not taught this form of "hearing" that I believe he's referring to. This listening to the deep. Listening to what we hear from within us. We have never been taught to listen to the feminine, to turn inward, to trust that dulcet voice that knows itself completely.

No one outside of you should ever be given the power to name you, or the burden of it. You carry the weight of knowing who you are. That is your responsibility and honor. When you know and name who you are, that is how time stops, how this moment right here goes back to the past and heals now what broke you back then.

There is no time in love. There is only intention. There is only the promise of redemption. When we let this love reach to where it has never been before, to where we are broken. This is when we reclaim what was always ours.

We are gifted this presence of the love inside us, and the first and last betrayal is the moment we stop listening. It's the moment we lose our faith in this presence that proves we are more than just our mistakes, we are more than just human.

This betrayal is ancient. Betrayal of the feminine is ingrained in the fabric of our belief. It's here, present in scripture from the 1st century. It's here at the start of Christianity. We question, we doubt, we disbelieve the feminine. We don't trust it. We don't feel it's worthy of our trust. We abandon the feminine; we bury it. We demonize it. We portray it, her, as a prostitute.

We forget that the feminine is a part of us. That the feminine is an essential half of what it means to be human and what it means to know god.

We forget that something eternal lives within us for as long as we draw breath. We forget that we are both male and female, masculine and feminine, light and dark, conscious and unconscious, human and angel, divine and animal. We forget that we are all actually undivided.

The Gospel of Thomas says, "Blessed are you in the midst of persecution who, when they hate and pursue you even to the core of your being, cannot find 'you' anywhere."

It's only the ego that suffers betrayal. This is why you are beyond words, and beyond any need to ever defend this eternity you hold in you. There is no 'you' that can ever be threatened.

What we have remembered is the other half of the story of Christ. We have remembered the love that can only come to life through us, from within. We have remembered her, the woman who knew Christ by heart.

The Woman with the Alabaster Jar

To be anointed with oil is higher than being immersed in water. It is when we are anointed, not when we are immersed in water, that we become Christians. Christ was called Messiah because of this: he is "the anointed one."

— The Gospel of Philip

What she has done will also be told in memory of her.

I was back from the pilgrimage and watching the first season of *The Crown* on Netflix. Binge watching, that is. I had spent most of that day for the time I had to write (while my son was at school) on compiling quotes about Mary Magdalene and her connection to anointing.

The episode I happened to watch was the one about the controversial televised coronation of Queen Elizabeth in 1953. The TV monitors are all switched off in the moment when the Archbishop approaches the Queen with the holy oil. This is the most sacred part of the ritual, we are told by the Duke of Windsor, the would-be king who abdicated the throne for his love of Wallis Simpson, an American socialite and divorcée.

He narrates to an audience of guests in his mansion in France as they take in all the complexities of the coronation. When someone asks why the anointing is the holiest part of the ceremony, too holy even for it to be televised, the former king explains that the anointing is the moment when the divine is infused into Elizabeth's human form. It's when she is no longer just Elizabeth, but Queen Elizabeth II. The holy oil marks that transformation from only human to now also divine.

The Archbishop hesitates before making the sign of the cross with the oil on her chest, and then her forehead. This is the part of the coronation that converts her from a woman into a queen.

The first time I came across the biblical passage about Mary Magdalene anointing Christ was in Jean-Yves Leloup's translation of her gospel. This is the translation with the painting by Giotto di Bondone of Mary Magdalene lifted up by angels above the mountain (which I can now say I climbed). This is the scene and legend that inspired my need to find her cave. An external depiction that for me is symbolic of what happened within her. The cave being her own heart.

Christ says in Matthew 26:13, "By pouring this perfume on me, she has prepared my body for burial." Leloup explains that Mary Magdalene walked the path of the sacred marriage. She demonstrates with her actions that she had become a bridge between the worlds. This act of anointing Christ's body couldn't have happened with just anyone. The fact that Mary was the one to have anointed Christ is a fact that marks her profound significance.

What she has done will also be told in memory of her.

That day we found the cave, after a teary good-bye with Alle Ooop, the Frenchman, and their beautiful teenaged kids, I called Veronique for a ride back from the café at the base of the mountain. Her husband answered and came to get me. As we made our way down the winding road that leads back into town, he told me that supposedly, on the day Mary Magdalene died, she came down from the cave in the mountains to the town of Saint-Maximin. He said she had given Saint Maximin a vision of her descent.

So, Saint Maximin was waiting there for Mary at the entrance to the town. And as soon as she arrived, Saint Maximin rushed to her, and she fell into his arms. There's a monument to mark where she died. It's just there on the side of the road. He stopped the car so I could get out and look at it. It's a large stone pillar with Mary Magdalene at the top of it being lifted up by four angels. I pressed my hand to it and closed my eyes. I thanked him and asked to go to her cathedral, Saint-Maximin. The icon I found of her then in the gift shop is the one of Mary Magdalene holding an alabaster jar.

The alabaster jar Mary holds in so many of the paintings and icons of her is filled with the holy oil used to anoint the body before burial. This, Leloup believes, reveals that Mary Magdalene understands how to master the transition of death: "Her appearances with special oils to use in anointing Jesus Christ place her in the tradition of priests and priestesses of Isis, whose unguents were used to achieve the transition over the threshold of death while retaining consciousness."[45]

In John 12:1–8, Christ defends Mary's use of the expensive spikenard to anoint him. When Judas is horrified that she wastes such an excessive amount of oil that could have been sold and the money given to the poor, Christ says, "It was intended that she should save this oil for the day of my burial." *It was intended.* This was not an act Mary did on a whim. She didn't just suddenly spill a year's worth of wages in oil onto Christ's feet for the hell of it. This was intentional. This was what had been intended all along.

Anointing is still the most sacred aspect of ritual in the Christian tradition. But we have forgotten the memory of the woman who made it sacred.

The Gospel of Philip explains the power of the holy oil to convert a human into the divine: "The name Christian is welcomed with anointing, in the fullness and energy of the cross, which the apostles call the union of opposites; then one is not just Christian, one is the Christ."[46] What's the union of opposites? Think of every binary that comes to mind: male and female, light and dark, human and divine, life and death. The union of opposites comes when you've reached a state of consciousness that allows you to integrate them both.

The ego seeks to divide and separate. Which is important, crucial even, if you want to arrive at work on time and fully dressed or write checks with your accurate name signed on them. The ego rocks in that department. And if you want to distinguish yourself as the one to blame or the one who is entirely blameless in the breakdown of a relationship, the ego reigns. Only the ego can identify the opposites. Only the soul knows the union of them both.

To be an anointed Christian, in this context, means to live with the consciousness of this union.

And if we see the resurrection narrative as a metaphor, the anointing ritual becomes the passage from the death of the ego, the limited self, "the egoic operating system," as Cynthia Bourgeault refers to it, into the expansive realm of the soul. This is the transformation of consciousness at the heart of the Christian tradition, and Mary Magdalene is the one who has shown us the way.

Anointing, then, in its original context, was the act of consciously acknowledging that the physical body passes away, but the soul within the body does not. Bourgeault believes that, "To reclaim anointing in its original context would make it the sacramental centerpiece of a whole new vision of Christianity based on spiritual transformation and the alchemy of love."[47]

After Mary anoints Christ with the spikenard and washes his feet with her hair, before his crucifixion, Christ says in Matthew 26:6–13: "Truly I tell you, wherever this gospel is preached in all the world, *what she has done will also be told in memory of her.*"

The Language of the Angels

If the Savior considered her to be worthy, who are you to disregard her?
For he knew her completely and loved her steadfastly.

— Mary 10:9–10

Like the mystic Marguerite Porete, we have so much of what Joan of Arc actually said, her real words, because of a lengthy trial leading up to her death. It's because of these transcripts from the trial we know details about her life before she became a legend: for example, that Joan would have preferred to stay home spinning wool. She never intended to be anything more than what was expected of a peasant girl in rural France in the early 15th century when she was born.

I often imagine the moment when Joan of Arc cut her hair. She was 13. And because of a vision she had of the archangel Michael, she cut her hair short, dressed in men's armor, and led the army in several campaigns that shifted the Hundred Years' War in France's favor.

"I die for speaking the language of the angels," Joan said. She had succeeded in every battle she was a part of. She wasn't on trial because of treason or war crimes charged against her. She wasn't even (ultimately) on trial for the reason they gave her: repeat offenses of cross-dressing. She was on trial because she had listened to a voice inside her, a voice that transcended the sex and gender roles of rural France in 1430. She spoke the language of the angels, which has no ceiling and no limit to the possibilities of what we can be in this lifetime.

This is why she was burned at the stake, not because she dressed like a man, which she did, but because she listened to the voice of love inside her, and she believed it enough to let it guide her.

The church declared Joan of Arc guilty of cross-dressing in 1431 and burned her at the stake. Supposedly, her last words were, "Hold the cross so high that I may see it through the flames."

Twenty-five years later, her mother demanded a retrial. Joan of Arc was declared innocent in 1456. And Pope Benedict canonized her a saint in 1920.

I don't know what the language of the angels sounded like exactly, for Joan. But if I had to guess, I'd say it's about hearing what's already in the heart and then declaring, even if you're terrified, "I am not afraid. I was born to do this," like Saint Joan did.

Joan of Arc is the girl who had the courage and the steel-like faith to follow the voice of an angel only she could hear, from within her. That voice cut her free from any expectations projected onto her in the world that she was born into. That voice connected her to her own inner world.

She was burned at the stake for speaking the language of the angels, which meant following that voice within her, that no one else could control or contain. That voice that only she could validate and act on. "Act, and God acts," she said.

This is where worth comes in.

What can block that voice, that language of the heart, the vision of love that's within us, is an ancient misunderstanding that we're not worthy of such proximity to an angel. It's that ancient divide, the idea that there is humanity and then there is divinity. That the two are separate, and what's more, that one is higher, more crucial, or more holy than the other.

The powers of the ego, the seven powers that we have moved through in Mary's gospel, are about a power *over.* But this language, this vision, is about a power *with.* It's about a love that comes from understanding the worth inherent in being human. A love that comes from experiencing that *"every nature, every modeled form, every creature, exists in and with each other."* Act and god acts; this is a living exchange. A constant dialogue. A mercy.

Who are we to disregard that voice of love?

Levi, in Mary 10:10, reminds Peter that Christ considered her worthy. *"For he knew her completely and loved her steadfastly."* So how could Peter disregard her? And how could we?

Now, let's imagine for a moment that nothing in any gospel has ever been literal. Let's imagine that it's meant to be poetic and suggestive. That all scripture is meant to point us through parable after parable to an awakening that can only come from within.

Then the cross can represent the interstice, the meeting point of all opposites. The place that's out beyond life and death, male and female, light and dark, human and divine, heaven and hell. The cross can be the holy instant when we can finally see who we truly are. "Hold the cross so high that I may see it through the flames."

We are not this struggle, this heartbreak. We are not this triumph, this drive to win. We are not the impulse to cause pain, or the compulsion to save lives. We are the moment when we think we are forsaken, forgotten. The moment when we think we are alone. And from out of the darkness a voice calls our name. And we remember.

Love is stronger than death.

In disregarding Mary, in forgetting who she was to Christ, *"For he knew her completely and loved her steadfastly,"* we disregard the aspect within us that's fluent with the angels.

We forget that actually Christ did not die alone on the cross; there was one who never left, who was with him from within her heart. There was a woman who could perceive his soul.

Remember. She wept at seeing the tomb empty. She needed to be with his body. She was there when no one else was. She was the love that remained.

She wept, and also there at the tomb she spoke to two angels. In place of where Christ's body had been, Mary saw, like Joan, two angels cloaked in white. (Remember, they appeared within her.) They asked her, "Why are you weeping?" Then Mary turns, and Christ asks her the same question as the angels, "Why are you weeping?" (Because love is stronger than death.)

This is what has been hidden from us. A love that is a power we have always been worthy of. A love that is a power *with* us, from within us. A love that brings us back to life, again and again.

The Prayer of the Heart

What is your inside is your outside,
And what you see on the outside,
You see revealed on the inside.

— THE THUNDER, PERFECT MIND 4:30–31

I was in full-on mom-mode. It's a mode that feels like a possession, like I've morphed into a cyclone. Cleaning up as if I had seven arms and calling out directives at my son as if we were suddenly under some sort of deadline to get everything organized in his room, as if we were about to get judged by some galactic panel that comes down hard on the messy and disheveled.

Then, suddenly, Shai belted out from across the room, with as much angst as Foreigner themselves, that classic '80s chorus of wanting to know what love is.

This, of course, cracked me up. He was communicating, with such levity and with that little twinkle in his eye, that he was feeling ordered around right now, not loved. So, I replied by singing the next line to the chorus, with matching angst and strain in my face, begging to know what love is, and wanting someone to show me.

He has skillful means at such a young age. With one lyric, he snaps me out of the trance of who I don't have to be.

I tackled him onto the bed and started kissing his cheeks like a crazy puppy until those peals of laughter I love so much came from him, dismantling the energy in the room the same way rays of light breaking through thick cloud cover shift the landscape. I returned to myself again. Not a mom primarily. Not a form-fitting, knowable thing. Not a revered or a hallowed thing. Just a human woman who loves with all her being this miraculous human who came from her own body.

Later that day, when Shai was with his dad, I went to a yoga class at the studio I love, called Inner Bliss. I love yoga. I do very little of it. I am adept at child's pose. I spend half the class in it. And I often enter Shavasana, the corpse pose, about a half hour before everyone else does. I've never felt the need to actually go into whatever next pose the teacher leads us through. Everything feels like a suggestion. It feels like church for me, body church. It's a place to be present, in my body, with a whole bunch of other bodies. A place to listen. And to rest my head on my stinky yoga mat and just let all my thoughts go. And do whatever helps me hear that voice that's always here with me, within me, ceaselessly telling me the love I know.

I stayed seated even after all the other budding yogis pushed back into their first of a billion downward dogs. I stayed rooted, sitting cross-legged on my mat, pretending my spine extended down, deep into the earth, reaching all the way to the underside of Australia, and that a ray of light shot up from the crown of my head, blinding the angels billions of light years away.

I tried to see my body as the world tree.

And of course, both places, all the way down and all the way up, are right here inside the heart. I took a deep breath, and I felt that descent, inward. And then I took a second breath to feel connected, and once I did, I whispered, "Where am I divided?" Instead of an answer, I felt compelled to open my eyes and start to move. So I met the class where they were—plank position. I planked, and asked again as I noticed the tension mounting in my neck, "Where am I divided?"

There was a super-duper handsome yogi man on my left. He was so attractive it sounded as if a slight gong noise emanated from his chest. We were asked to do the cat-cow pose next. I went into the X-rated version. Craning my neck up far enough that my mouth opened ever so slightly and tilting my pelvis to an unnatural degree. On my third time through, I felt a sharp tweak of pain. I had overcocked my coccyx. I yelped. The pain was like a slap. Wake up! I was aware then that I was cat-cowing the hell out of my body for the sake of the handsome yogi man beside me. Who, of course, hadn't even noticed. I started to laugh.

How human of me. A wide Cheshire-cat smile took over my face. I whispered again, now with this levity and pulsating joy, "Where am I divided?"

The song ended and a new song began right then. A voice I adore, Krishna Das. A voice that goes back to when I first fell in love with yoga, at divinity school, while studying the Divine Feminine, Tantra, Isis, and finding Mary's gospel, all while beginning to understand that no matter how many sacred texts I read, I will never learn more than when I'm able to just be fully present in my body.

It was a chant by Krishna Das I hadn't heard before. And as we moved slowly into Warrior One pose, I heard Krishna Das sing the chorus Shai had just belted out to me earlier that day, from Foreigner, about wanting to know what love is. My smile got even wider.

I know this state so well. This state of grace, where everything is so loud and clear and so entirely in my face. Where the message of what's here to learn, to take in, presents itself in these curious sympathies, these "synchronicities," as Carl Jung would call them. I sang quietly along with Krishna Das as he continued chanting his Kirtan to god, about wanting to feel what love is, and knowing "you" (god) can show me. I had prayed myself right into the experience of the answer.

When things align like this, I remember what union might mean, as if in a dream I had recently. I can't articulate the details with any precision; it's more of a fleeting feeling that seems to slip in and out of my grasp like a spirited fish with slippery skin. It's this feeling of integrity, where what's within me is outside of me. Where who I am, all that I am, is right here, present.

And what I think and feel comes through me, effortlessly, with no filtering and no holding back. Where the love within me expands out in widening circles; where I'm aware that I hold love within me, and that I am held in love from outside of me.

Where I'm in love. And this lets me feel (even if just momentarily) the bliss of continuity, of being undivided from my heart to my words, and thoughts, to how my body moves and breathes. It's all unified and undivided. *I'm* unified. *I'm* undivided.

This is how I understand this passage from *The Thunder, Perfect Mind*, "What is your inside is your outside, and what you see on the outside, you see revealed on the inside." The alchemist dictum, "as above, so below," points to this same truth. If the world within us is bound to the ego, we will see a world outside of us through that lens. And if the world within us is freed to see with the eyes of the soul, then we see things as they truly are; we will see the heaven that's already here. Nowhere else but in this humble, frequently humiliated, utterly shattered human heart.

This is the singleness I believe Christ reached and Mary followed. And this to me is what made her the first apostle or, if you prefer, the apostle to the apostles. This capacity to become undivided. As Cynthia Bourgeault explains, "Apostleship does not lie in having been near Jesus, taught or studied with him, or attended the Last Supper. It lies in the inner integration (singleness) which allows that person to live in continuous communion with the Master in the imaginal meeting ground through the power of a pure heart, so that 'Thy Kingdom come' is in fact a living reality."[48]

This, to me, is the perfect human, the *anthropos* that Christ in Mary's gospel calls us all to be. We are to clothe ourselves with this holy mix of being an ego, a self that struggles every single day to cope, and also equally, a soul that is eternal and knows it, a soul that is love and never needs to prove it. And this is the state I can keep choosing to be in, that I can practice returning to faster.

Yes, I'm here in a state with a slogan, "the heart of it all," my home state that has asked me to heal all the way back and all the way through. Ultimately, I'm here, in my body, in this cathedral heart that's all lit up with a love that has never left. I have died to the ego's idea of me, which is something I keep doing, daily. I have replaced an eye for an eye, a hand for a hand, so that what I see blazes.

This is why everything has changed and everything has stayed the same, because what has always been here in my heart is now met, fully. What I knew might exist, does. My inside is my outside. This is what the gospel of Mary Magdalene gave to me—the confirmation of what my body has always told me. There's another way to see what it means to be human and god all at once. Like a yolk in an egg, like a soul in a body, like a world within a world, that begins and never ends.

AFTERWORD

I Believe Mary

We should clothe ourselves with the perfect Human, acquire it for ourselves as he commanded us, and announce the Good news.

— **Mary 10:11–13**

Now that we've heard about what has been hidden from us, the last passage from the Gospel of Mary answers what we can each do to acquire "the perfect Human" for ourselves.

Personally, the word *perfect* makes me cringe.

I much prefer the word *complete* or *true* in its place. True as in whole. Authentic. Integral. So, we are to clothe ourselves with the true human. And this means that once we have stripped ourselves of the stories and ideas that feed the raging fires of the ego, or the power to judge (which ensnares us in a cycle of the ego's seven powers), then the only thing we should put back on is this understanding or vision of being a true human being, the self and the soul united.

This, of course, does not mean we remain that way. Perfect, whole, unified, complete. It does not mean we are infallible, and incorruptible, and that we float from now on several feet above the ground. It doesn't mean we have to always wear white, never have sex, and abstain from anything that would actually make us happy. All of these ideas of perfect have confused us about what it means to be spiritual, to be a spiritually grown-up and true human being.

As humans, we forget, as Mary revealed to us. The chains of forgetfulness bind us again to the ego. The work we're being called to here, though, is to "clothe ourselves with the perfect Human." So we have to do the work that allows us to remember, again and again, and with greater ease and levity, this experience of the self as also a soul. This experience of not just being this pain, and grief, and terror of the ego, but also this soul of love that loves through us.

This love that whispers from within us, when we are exhausted and alone, *"Give to me what you cannot carry."*

We are to "acquire it for ourselves as he commanded us," which translates to me as seeing Christ as an example, a way-shower, a trail-blazer in what it means to be human.

This doesn't speak of idolizing or worshipping or distancing Christ from us or from what it means to be human. This says he commanded us to try, as we are each able, to experience the truth that he realized, which is that within the human heart sits a treasure. That treasure will be referred to as a diamond, as a light that pierces all other light, as heaven, as gold by the alchemists, as the soul, as the aspect of us that's inseparable from god.

If we can "acquire it," since it's already ours, and since it's already here within us, then we will be able to see (thanks to the nous, the eye of the heart) that we are not separate from it. That we are no greater or less than a mustard seed, a tree, a flower, a wolf, a star, an angel, those streaks of red in a sunset that takes the breath away. We are aware, again, of what we had forgotten, that everything *"exists in and with each other."* And this is humbling and empowering all at once.

Because when I speak, if I speak from this place, from this treasure that has been hidden from us, then I use a voice that is more than my own. I become a voice in service of love. I become that one unified voice that demanded Thecla's freedom. It's a voice that's more like fire, like an invisible flame that inconspicuously meets us in that silence inside us and asks us to be brave enough to tell the truth.

This is how, for me at least, I can "announce the Good news," as a voice in service of love.

The good news that god is, simply, Good, that god is not male or female, or removed from us, high above and beyond our comprehension. God is simply the good, which exists within, and between, each one of us.

The good news that there is no such thing as sin. We have nothing to be ashamed of in being human, in having a body, in feeling all that this body knows, which is lost to the intellect and beyond reason.

We have nothing to be ashamed of or to ever have to hide when it comes to who we love. Who we love is not determined by our body or theirs, not their sex or their gender but the soul that expresses itself through it all.

And the authority for speaking on behalf of this love comes from the depth of the transformation a person has undergone within themselves to remember who they really are.

It is determined by their proximity to this experience of love, to this treasure Christ commands us to find. And that proximity to love lets them emanate humility, because they know in their bones the radical worth and equality of us all. It lets them radiate mercy, an almost freakish amount of giving all their love away. Giving their love to anyone and everyone, knowing as they do, that the more they give, the more they receive from within the heart. *Lord Jesus Christ, son of god, have mercy on me.* Mercy is this exchange, this law of the universe.

Announcing is not converting; it's not proselytizing. *Cor ad cor loquitur.* Heart speaks to heart directly. Those who have two ears will be able to hear and understand. It's our work to do what we can to remember the soul, to remember the love that's at the heart of how and why we heal.

It's our work to undo the systems of power that confuse us into forgetting our own power.

The good news to me is that true power rests within us. That like Mary Magdalene, like Thecla, Perpetua, Joan of Arc, Marguerite Porete, and Theresa of Avila demonstrated, no one outside of us can keep us from finding this power. Because it's not a power over us or outside of us. It's a power that rests within us, and we can rest in it, be led by it, and be carried by it.

It's a power that takes us breath by breath, if we let it, to the places where our ego's the loudest and most afraid, so we can become aware of the contrast; the stark contrast between the world the ego sees and the world love sees.

It's a power that's the opposite of power. It's love. And it's this love that frees us from the ego so we can hear what's in the heart, and then tell the truth.

And that might sound too daunting. Telling the truth. Let me call on Hemingway here. When I get overwhelmed with what I'm going to write, or how in the hell I could ever say what feels like a symphony inside me, I freeze up, and cry, and spend most of the day cleaning the floor or the toilets so I don't have to face my own ineptitude. To start writing again, I turn to Hemingway's reminder; "All you have to do is write one true sentence. Write the truest sentence that you know." We just have to tell each next truth we hear from within. And this is what frees us from the very unique cages our own egos have constructed for us.

The perfect, or true human, is anchored into this love, and also, is equally, still and for as long as we have a body, this raging ego that will resist the "death" this love demands. So, it's all part of the process. It's part of what it means to be spiritual, and to be "perfect," and to be an absolute mess at times. To fall flat on our egos and scream, for example, while sobbing in the shower. Or to storm out of a situation you couldn't possibly handle calmly in the moment.

The good news is that it's just alpha, and then omega, ad infinitum. It's just a constant return. A myriad of opportunities to come back to this voice of love inside us. And we can spend less and less time away from it, or feeling as though we're separate from it, or aren't worthy of it, if we choose to. Being human isn't the failure. Being human is the soul's chance to be here.

The guru, the saint, the magi, the "perfected" ideal of yourself that can radiate beams of light like Princess Fiona after Shrek's true love kiss, and remain that way, is an illusion. This is often used as a way for us to feel inadequate. To constantly compare ourselves. To constantly suggest to ourselves that we're not there yet. We haven't arrived.

The good news is we never arrive. None of us. Not even the holiest person you can think of in this moment, like Oprah or the Dalai Lama. We never get there. That's the whole point of being human. The point is to constantly arrive. For some of us with each breath. We constantly return to love. This is the good news; that we can. That it's set up this way. That no matter who we are or how long we've been separated from feeling the presence of love, it's actually right here.

Within.

I came across an article recently published in *Harvard Magazine* about Dr. Karen King and her translation of Mary's gospel, titled, "The Bits the Bible Left Out." Dr. King says it occurred to her that, "the central point of the gospel wasn't the dispute between disciples, but the rise of the soul."[49] King explains, "The more I thought about it, the more the gospel seemed to be about a spiritual path in this life as much as what might happen in the afterlife."[50]

An ascent narrative, a story about the rise of the soul, this is at the heart of the Gospel of Mary. For me, what I've come to understand is that it's the soul that rises, not me, not my ego, not anything "human" that I am. The soul rises up from within me. It's the soul that rises. And I descend inward to meet it. Does that make sense? The soul rises up from within the heart and we have the chance, again and again, if we can get still and present enough to just listen.

And we don't have to wait until death to encounter the soul. The soul is right here. Like our own private heaven inside us. We can choose to die now and live as someone who has walked through death like Mary, and chose to resurrect as someone who cannot be separate from love.

Your inside will be your outside.

If you can listen to the silence inside you, hear what love wants you to say, to do, then no one outside of you can ever silence you again.

And, for me, each time I do this, no matter how small or insignificant the truth I hear, even if it's just a quiet, unassuming "yes" to attend an event, or a "no" to something someone is asking of me, I feel like I've triumphed. Like somehow, taking that voice seriously has an impact that reaches all the way back and all the way through to the time I was silenced as a little girl. That if I remember the worth of that quiet (fierce) unassuming voice of love inside me, I save myself. Each time I simply use it.

I guess it feels collective too. That it's not just a personal battle over my own demons I win when I listen to that voice and believe it enough to take action on it and do what's true for me, I also somehow move Mary's story forward. I heal the disbelief. I heal the ancient misunderstanding that I was ever unworthy, that you could ever be unworthy, that she was unworthy. In consciously listening for what's true for me and saying it, I practice the fact that I believe Mary.

I don't know what's next for me and Mary Magdalene. What I see, or imagine, is simple. There's this circle of us, this motley crew, and we're all trying to understand her gospel. Maybe we're a church, or a congregation of some sort that has included all the bits the bible left out. And we try, imperfectly together, to practice and know the kind of radical love her heart was capable of.

Can you see it? Maybe we'll sit in the same circle at some point. Or maybe you'll start a circle wherever you are. Realizing, as you must by now, that you're as much an authority on Mary Magdalene as I am. Because you're an authority of the voice of your own soul. And because you remember that there is no hierarchy in the spiritual world.

Or if circles aren't for you, or you can't cross the distance to join one, just stay where you are. There's no distance love cannot cross. Just tie a red thread around your wrist. And go inward.

I'll leave you with this.

My ladylove, Kate (or the Good Witch, as Shai has called her since he was two), spent a weekend with me recently at a place called Omega. It was a sort of mom's soul camp slumber party. We came to see one of our favorite writers and her wife for a conference about living our truest lives. I was expecting to cry a lot because Kate and I always do. Our proximity to each other seems to amplify all of our emotions. And this, of course, makes our laughing harder too.

What I wasn't expecting were the jolts of sheer electricity that shot through me every time I saw the two presenters look at each other. Their love was visible. Palpable. My soul swooned. Each time I saw that light in their eyes zip like a tiny flash of lightning between them, my body seemed to erupt into an exuberant gospel choir, singing, "EVERYTHING'S STILL POSSIBLE."

We discussed the importance of women coming together, of letting our love for each other shift the current climate of divisiveness. That we can answer this time of alternate facts that incite violence with more unity, with an even louder, more radical love, and we can practice love more faithfully, as Dr. Cornel West describes, "Justice is what love looks like in public."

There was a lot of dancing, which to me has always felt like the way women pray when no else is watching. At one point, Pink's "I Am Here" came over the speakers and we all shot up like choreographed dancers into the aisles and between the chairs.

I thought as I danced of the picture my mom had taken of me and Tarana Burke, founder of the Me Too movement, earlier that week. It was taken right after I sobbed my thank-you to her brilliant, knowing eyes. I said to her, "I'm a survivor. I've never felt less alone. We're together now." And I thought of all the marches

I had joined recently, my one small raspy voice, among a sea of other voices, unified as if one mouth. I knew I was making my mother and great-grandmother proud, and also all the generations who had stood up through the centuries to love the other as themselves.

My eyes are so puffy and red in that picture. And the smile that's on my face, I've never looked more real. There's elation in it. There's this resilience. This victory. This tiny personal triumph.

This is what I felt as I danced with the Good Witch and about 300 other women, tears streaming down my face, ecstatic, screaming off-key but with the force of a declaration, "I Am Here." Here in a body with a sign above the door in my heart that reads, "Here anyone can live free."

We've seen the world that the ego creates in its insatiable quest to acquire material worth, power over others, and supremacy. What we have the possibility of cultivating is the world the soul creates. The world Christ and Mary and a radical band of believers in the 1st century wanted to realize. The ones who knew that the inner transformation creates the outer transformation. That the love that's hidden within each of us is the only power that can save all of us.

I thought of Penny, and the prayer of the heart she had taught me on that Buddhist retreat so long ago. How small and magnificent she was. And I realized that this is what her presence had said to me too, that everything was still possible. Or as the Nobel Peace Prize–nominated author and monk Thich Nhat Hanh relates, "Because you are alive, everything is possible."

I think my elation came from this: There was no part of me that was "existing elsewhere." I was here with a radical band of believers. We're all still here. The names and the dates change. But the love never ends.

On the last night of the retreat, Kate and I (in matching jammies) rolled up the imaginary window between our beds (so we'd stop talking) and said our good-nights early to get some sleep.

I pulled up the covers and proceeded to have the least restful night of my life. Here I was at a place called Omega, which is the last letter in the Greek alphabet, or the end, and here's what it felt like: I closed my eyes and I walked, wide-awake, into a pitch-dark classroom. It felt like I was entering kindergarten, no, preschool. I was starting all over. I was at the beginning again.

My heart started to swell with this ineffable light. No, it's not a light, it's a warmth. No, it's more than the feeling of warmth, it's the absence of emptiness. It's a sensation of finally reaching a place you realize in a very real way you have never left. You just know now, you're here. This is where you are in reality. Right here, in the dark, in the presence of the light that has never left you. And as you let your heart swell, all you can see is a hand reaching out toward you. You don't need to know what's next, when what's next comes from within. You just remain. You just reach out to take this hand that is always extending out toward you and you start again.

You hear Joan of Arc say, "I am not afraid; I was born to do this." You hear Marguerite Porete say, "Love has no beginning, no end, and no limit, and I am nothing except love." You hear Perpetua say, "Love one another." You hear Thecla say, "In the name of Jesus Christ, I baptize myself." And, you hear Mary Magdalene say, "I will teach you about what is hidden from you."

And this is how you rise; further up is farther in. And the darkness is where the light has always been. Here in the heart is the treasure. And you remember again and again, *I am here.*

APPENDIX 1

The Soul-Voice Meditation

The soul-voice meditation is a practice I created from my exposure to the history of Christian contemplative prayer while in seminary, specifically in the form of the Byzantine mystics known as Hesychasts. Hesychastic practice originates in the Eastern Orthodox Church and dates back to at least as early as the 4th century. It was an exclusively eremitic tradition that involved the metaphysical and physio-spiritual process of turning inward and focusing only on the heart in order to experience the divine directly. This spiritual process is recounted in detail by Evagrius Pontikos in *The Sayings of the Desert Fathers* in the 4th century and then again two centuries later in Saint John of Sinai's *The Ladder of Divine Ascent.*

Hesychia is Greek for stillness, rest, and silence. Hesychasm was a contemplative practice for hermits and male monastics to go within and meet with that voice that doesn't need words. The voice beneath the voice of the ego. The soul-voice. I am quite clearly the antithesis to a 4th-century male monastic. I was, however, somewhat of an urban nun after three years of seminary. And the ancient Hesychast and I had one pivotal commonality, a red thread that bound us: the desire to always be aware of the divine.

So I took the spiritual tool the Heschasts provided of turning inward and of focusing all of my attention into a space called "heart," a space of limitless truth inside me. And I began a daily meditation practice of going inward, to open to that stillness in the heart, and to the presence of my soul that would never fail to meet me there.

It doesn't matter where I am or what I'm doing or who I happen to be with at the time. Like Kegels, no one has to know I'm even doing it for it to be effective. It can be very cloak-and-dagger, meditating. No incense needed, no closed eyes even. I mean, I prefer it, but I've had powerful SVMs on the elliptical machine at the gym, or while driving. Going inward is all about the intention that's set, not about the setting that's surrounding me.

What I found from my own practice over the past decade is that it allows me to know one invaluable thing: my own truth. It lets me hear my own voice, even amid the pressures of external expectations, or especially, internalized ones.

The quote that received the most attention from my first book, *REVEAL*, came from the Soul-Voice chapter and reads: "There will never be a voice outside of you that is wiser than your soul-voice or holds more authority over what is best for you. You need guidance and support not to follow someone else's truth but to remain loyal to your own. The voice that will guide you to your highest potential is within you."[51]

The soul-voice meditation is a spiritual tool for seekers of all religious traditions to be able to go within no matter where they are and connect to the voice of truth inside them. It's a tool that helps them discern between the voice of fear and the voice of love. That sounds wildly simplistic. But I've found that it really is simple. I've found that we tend to already know the answers to the questions we're seeking. Fear creates this static or white noise and this jittery, frenetic energy that makes us think we can (a) find the answer outside of us, and (b) find the answer with the mind. The answer, however, in my experience, doesn't come from a thought, it comes from a feeling. And we have access to those feelings in the heart. Heart, as in, again, that limitless (and somewhat) fathomless space within us where we can meet with what is far more than our own ego's life-span.

Start by taking a deep breath, and with this breath set the intention to go into your heart. Imagine this space called heart however you want to—a cathedral with light-drenched stained-glass windows, a disco ball hanging above a dance floor casting light diamonds everywhere as it spins, a little red raft on a warm, calm ocean that just floats and sustains you and feels like the most dependable thing that has ever existed.

Then, when you're there (and by there I mean when you feel as though you've settled yourself enough to go inward, when you feel that state of heart that only comes from dislodging the mind, or that feeling that comes when you cut yourself off from thoughts of the past and concerns of the future, and you're just sort of hanging out, right here), take a second breath. And with this second breath set the intention of meeting with your soul, and if soul scares you, set the intention of meeting with your truth, and if the word *truth* sounds unapproachable, just intend to meet with love. And if you're afraid to meet with love (who isn't), then just intend to meet with your voice. That one you had at some point in your life, like when you wore a cape at age seven, or when you stood up to that bully on the playground in middle school, or when you told that first crush how you actually felt, or when you said that first no to someone you wanted to impress but had to get real instead, or when you said that first yes even though you knew it meant that others would judge you and not understand. That voice. Take your second intentional breath and with it run to that voice like it's your long-lost beloved. Because it is.

Now, together, when you and this soul-voice have linked pinkies again, or are walking arm in arm in your imagination, or heart-cathedral, or floating together on a little red raft on the calmest seas that have never existed, then *ask*. Ask anything and everything. And here's the most important thing ever, *believe* it. Believe this voice you hear inside you so much that you actually act on it. Believe in this voice. Believe in you.

Before taking the third breath, start to give gratitude. Say thank-yous like throwing confetti at a wedding. Thank everything and anything that might have come to you. Because what we ask inwardly, we find.

Let me break down briefly what it means to speak the language of the angels, like Mary Magdalene, or Theresa of Avila, or Joan of Arc. We don't have to be legends or religion-starting figures in history to hear them. "Angels," to me, are those moments when I can hear something new, when I can see a circumstance or person differently. When I can take off the lens of how I was seeing myself and see through that illusion to the reality. And this new vision then frees me.

So, "seeing" comes in many forms. And the way it will come to you is the way most often that will freak you out the least. So, for example, in REDLADIES, some ladies hear their soul-voice in an actual "voice." In that internal voice only we can hear within us. Others "hear" their soul-voice through these images that appear in the wake of whatever question they have asked, and this image tells them a story, which contains the answers. And some feel the response. Some just ask and know because of a flood of emotion that just communicates what words and images cannot. That bone knowing, that unspoken truth that just flashes us a peek at the universe and then hides itself again in the mystery.

With this third breath, intend to surface from behind your eyes, seeing out now with the eyes of love. There's nothing more radical or revolutionary than doing this every day.

APPENDIX 2

Mary Magdalene's Red Thread Reading List

Beyond Belief: The Secret Gospel of Thomas, by Elaine Pagels (New York: Vintage Books, May 2004).

The Gospel of Mary Magdalene, by Jean-Yves Leloup (Rochester, VT: Inner Traditions, 2002).

The Gospel of Mary of Magdala: Jesus and the First Woman Apostle, by Karen L. King (Santa Rosa, CA: Polebridge Press, 2003).

The Gospel of Philip: Jesus, Mary Magdalene, and the Gnosis of Sacred Union, by Jean-Yves Leloup (Rochester, VT: Inner Traditions, 2003).

Holy Blood, Holy Grail, by Michael Baigent, Richard Leigh, and Henry Lincoln (New York: Random House, 1982).

The Meaning of Mary Magdalene: Discovering the Woman at the Heart of Christianity, by Cynthia Bourgeault (Boulder, CO: Shambhala, 2010).

A New New Testament: A Bible for the 21st Century Combining Traditional and Newly Discovered Texts, edited by Hal Taussig (New York: Houghton Mifflin Harcourt, 2013).

The Pistis Sophia, edited and translated by G. R. S. Mead (New York: Cambridge University Press, 2012).

The Red Book, by C. G. Jung, translated by Mark Kyburz, John Peck, and Sonu Shamdasani (New York: Philemon Foundation and W. W. Norton & Company, 2009).

The Resurrection of Mary Magdalene: Legends, Apocrypha, and the Christian Testament, by Jane Schaberg (New York: The Continuum International Publishing Group, 2002).

The Sacred Embrace of Jesus and Mary: The Sexual Mystery at the Heart of the Christian Tradition, by Jean-Yves Leloup (Rochester, VT: Inner Traditions, 2005).

The Serpent's Gift: Gnostic Reflections on the Study of Religion, by Jeffrey Kripal (Chicago: The University of Chicago Press, 2007).

The Wisdom Jesus: Transforming Heart and Mind—A New Perspective on Christ and His Message, by Cynthia Bourgeault (Boulder, CO: Shambhala, 2008).

Writings from the Philokalia on Prayer of the Heart, translated by Kadloubovsky and Palmer (New York: Faber & Faber, Inc., 1979).

APPENDIX 3

Resources for Giving and Receiving Support

Me Too Movement
www.metoomvmt.org

VDAY
www.vday.org

Love146
www.love146.org

Together Rising
www.togetherrising.org

ENDNOTES

Why I Could Kiss a Copt

1. Cynthia Bourgeault, *The Wisdom Jesus: Transforming Heart and Mind—A New Perspective on Christ and His Message* (Boulder, CO: Shambhala, 2008), 16.

2. Karen L. King, *The Gospel of Mary of Magdala: Jesus and the First Woman Apostle* (Santa Rosa, CA: Polebridge Press, 2003), 11.

3. Cynthia Bourgeault, *The Meaning of Mary Magdalene: Discovering the Woman at the Heart of Christianity* (Boulder, CO: Shambhala, 2010), 44.

4. Hal Taussig, ed., *A New, New Testament: A Bible for the 21st Century Combining Traditional and Newly Discovered Texts* (New York: Houghton Mifflin Harcourt Company, 2013), 100.

How a Feminist Sees an Angel

5. King, *The Gospel of Mary of Magdala*, 152.

Grandma Betty's Lightbulb Eyes

6. Ibid., 160.

7. Ibid.

8. Jean-Yves Leloup, *The Gospel of Mary Magdalene* (Rochester, VT: Inner Traditions, 2002), xi.

9. Ibid., 20.

The Buddha Tara's Badass Vow

10. Jean-Yves Leloup, *The Gospel of Philip: Jesus, Mary Magdalene, and the Gnosis of Sacred Union* (Rochester, VT: Inner Traditions, 2003).

11. Bourgeault, *The Meaning of Mary Magdalene*, 115.

12. Pistis Sophia II, 72, quoted in Schaberg, *The Resurrection*, 162, and Kripal's *The Serpent's Gift*, 56.

The Gospel of Mary Magdalene

13. Leloup, *The Gospel of Mary Magdalene*, 72.

What It Means to Be Saved

14. Bourgeault, *The Wisdom Jesus*, 17.

15. Ibid., 19.

16. Ibid., 21.

What It Means to Be Human

17. Leloup, *The Gospel of Philip*, 27.

18. Jean-Yves Leloup, *The Sacred Embrace of Jesus and Mary: The Sexual Mystery at the Heart of the Christian Tradition* (Rochester, VT: Inner Traditions, 2005), 37.

19. Bourgeault, *The Meaning of Mary Magdalene*, 107.

20. Leloup, *The Sacred Embrace of Jesus and Mary*, 8.

What I Learned as the Burning Bush

21. *Writings from the Philokalia on Prayer of the Heart*, trans. Kadloubovsky and Palmer (New York: Faber and Faber, Inc., 1979), 28.

22. Ibid., 30.

23. Ibid., 38.

24. Ibid., 119.

How to Meditate Like Mary Magdalene

25. Taussig, *A New, New Testament*, xiii.

26. Leloup, *The Gospel of Mary Magdalene*, 14.

27. Bourgeault, *The Meaning of Mary Magdalene*, 60.

28. Ibid., 71.

29. *Writings from the Philokalia on Prayer of the Heart*, 38.

Mary Magdalene Was Not a Prostitute

30. Bourgeault, *The Meaning of Mary Magdalene*, Preface.

31. Leloup, *The Gospel of Mary Magdalene*, xiv.

32. King, *The Gospel of Mary of Magdala*, 152

33. Ibid.

34. Ibid., 144.

35. Ibid.

36. Leloup, *The Gospel of Philip*.

A Religion Every Body Belongs To

37. Bourgeault, *The Meaning of Mary Magdalene*, 65.

Why I Am Proud to Be Part Impala

38. Peter Levine, *Waking the Tiger: Healing Trauma* (Berkeley: North Atlantic Books, 1997), 20.

A Ship Without Sails

39. I met with all these people in a dream; they were standing in a semicircle in front of me. Their faces were the most endearing faces I had ever seen. No, it's more as if these were the faces of the people I've always loved. Or always sensed with me. Somehow within me, or within my heart. I felt this ache to see them standing there with me, before me. I felt home. They were a motley crew, a circuslike bunch of beloved friends. There was a tall, lanky man; his eyes were so kind and quiet, I started crying. There was a slight, sinewy woman standing beside him with the most eloquent hands. There was a childhood friend I only half-remembered; her name was Mo. And there was an imaginary friend who I had completely forgotten. His skin was red. I scanned their faces in the semicircle again and again. I wanted to keep the imprint of what it felt like to have them with me again; or to remember they'd never left. Then I told each one of them. Because I had realized that this was why they were here. I told each one that I had been assaulted as a little girl. And it hurt, physically, to tell them. To say it out loud. But it also got easier. It got lighter. And then I understood what was happening. They were carrying it with me. Because, I understood then, that this is what love does. Love takes for us what we can't carry alone.

The Princess of Mercy

40. Bourgeault, *The Meaning of Mary Magdalene*, 105

She Who Confirms the Truth

41. Leloup, *The Sacred Embrace of Jesus and Mary*, 106.

The White Spring

42. Elaine Pagels, *Beyond Belief: The Secret Gospel of Thomas* (New York: Vintage Books, 2004), Saying 37, 232.

43. Leloup, *The Gospel of Philip*.

44. Bourgeault, *The Meaning of Mary Magdalene*, 103.

The Woman with the Alabaster Jar

45. Leloup, *The Gospel of Mary Magdalene*, xxii.

46. Leloup, *The Gospel of Philip*.

47. Bourgeault, *The Meaning of Mary Magdalene*, 187.

The Prayer of the Heart

48. Bourgeault, *The Meaning of Mary Magdalene*, 68.

I Believe Mary

49. Lydialyle Gibson, "The Bits the Bible Left Out," *Harvard Magazine*, November–December 2018, 44.

50. Ibid.

The Soul-Voice Meditation

51. Meggan Watterson, *REVEAL: A Sacred Manual for Getting Spiritually Naked* (Carlsbad, CA: Hay House, 2011), 70.

ACKNOWLEDGMENTS

REDLADIES for the way we love and show up for each other, for letting me give my version of a sermon each month, for practicing the soul-voice meditation with me, and for daring to be vulnerable, and real, and to tell the truth together in service of love

Louise Hay & Reid Tracy for giving me the honor and privilege of writing this book

Patty Gift for being there at the first MNDFL teacher training when I started sharing the Gospel of Mary and the way she might have meditated, for always believing in me, for loving France as much as I do, and for knowing that I needed to write about Mary's gospel

Michelle Pilley for always seeing me, and for reminding me that the eagle is the ascended sign of the Scorpio

Anne Barthel for your kindness and immense patience, for your expert editing, and for your understanding the way I needed to go through a transformation myself as I wrote about the transformation Mary's gospel inspires

Kelly Notaras for reminding me that this was the book I was born to write

Terri Masi for those long walks on the beach in Montauk, for being sisters no matter what, and for being someone who can talk with me about Christ, and angels, and visions and women's rightful place in the church

Joseph Masi for that talk we had when I called after Omega, for always wanting to return to love, and most especially, for our gift

Margie & John Wheeler for teaching me about goodness, helping make a home for me and Shai in Cleveland so we could finally stay still, and for being there for Shai when I needed to go off and be a pilgrim again for the sake of my heart, soul, and this book

Andrew & Randy Watterson for all those Sunday dinners you invited me and Shai to while I was writing this book, offering him "fancy" white-tablecloth-type dining that I could never pull off, and for taking me in when he was away over Christmas

Elizabeth "Betty" Boyd for letting me talk about angels with you, and Christ, and all the things about god I didn't know who else to go to with, for being my pen pal, for helping me understand Christianity, and for coming to me that morning before I gave your eulogy

Elizabeth Wheeler for somehow always knowing when to call, for keeping my spirit light, for always being there, and for my Sophia Chia Pet

Shai Watterson Masi for asking my heart to perpetually expand to meet the amount of love you are, for "kiss alarms," for that bird whistle you blow when you want me to come running to cuddle, for your laugh that makes me laugh with you no matter what I'm feeling, for being the brightest most beautiful soul I know

David & Cathy Watterson for the unconditional love and support you give me

Gordon House for wisely and lovingly teaching me about the power of the circle and the history of the Navajo people

Wendi for what you could see long before I could, and always, for the red thread

Cheryl Richardson for that walk around the lake near your house when you had me listen with you to Marie Howe recite her poem "Magdalene Afterwards" and we both cried at the end of it and didn't need to explain why

Kate "Speed of Joy" Fisher for Just Love, and for sending me that wooden box with the world tree on it on the same day I found a dream catcher of the world tree, and also, just because

Christiane Northrup for unbinding my heart with me and our beloved Kyle, for our eco-hut, and Jazzercising, for knowing I needed a steak after my unexpected skinny-dip into the White Spring, and for reminding me that my love is here to be met

Table 1 on the *Queen Mary* for the lively conversations, for not making fun of my gluten-free status and how little I could eat while at sea, and for reminding me I'm never alone

Kristyn Gorton for coming down from Leeds to stay with me in London, for helping me with my earache, for snoring so loud I couldn't sleep and could only laugh

Robert & Hollie Holden for giving me a home base before and after my pilgrimage to find Mary's cave, for Bo's *Hallelujah*, and for seeing with me the love that has no beginning and has no end

Lyna Rose Jones for being Mary Magdalene sisters-in-love, for that dinner we had in Aix, for swapping MM devotion stories with me, for driving me to Saint-Maximin and helping me arrange my stay at the convent, for letting me go down to her crypt alone, for knowing that was exactly what I needed, and most of all, for telling me about the Cave of Eggs

Alle Ooop for literally saving my life on the side of that mountain, for praying with me to find Mary's Cave of Eggs, for reminding me of Toni Morrison's well-articulated truth "the function of freedom is to free someone else," and for sharing with me one of the best days of my life

Sonja Lockyer for inviting me to teach about the Gospel of Mary in the South of France, and for that skinny-dip late at night in a pool lined with wild lavender and the stars bright above us

Donna Freitas for meeting me in Paris, for teaching me about how to ask for what I want, and for the way you pray to Mary with your whole heart

Rebecca Campbell for inviting me to lead the soul-voice meditation with your retreat at the Chalice Well, for that dance we did together before it started to Meg Mac's "Roll Up Your Sleeves"

Rich & Lisa Lister for that hug Rich gave me that never quite ended, and for that song Lisa sang to me as I entered the White Spring and was never quite the same again

Ger for being in Devon with me, for revealing your extraordinary love, as you always do, for driving me from Devon to Glastonbury, and for that mixture of oils you made to calm my nerves for the flight home—I love you REDLADY

Claire Quartel and the ladies in Devon for inviting me to lead a circle about Mary Magdalene and the soul-voice meditation, for being so brave, for sharing what's true, for dancing together, and for loving that sparrow as much as I did

Lodro Rinzler for inviting me to be the Christian meditation teacher for MNDFL's teacher training, where this book was conceived

Latham Thomas for holding out for the beloved with me, for inviting me to lead The Divine Feminine Oracle in your gorgeous Circle

Gabrielle Bernstein for that divinely timed FaceTime, for reminding me of the light that never goes out even when it's darkest, and for being the most generous soul I know

Danielle LaPorte & Rochelle Schieck for sending me Mary Magdalene swag from Sainte-Baume and Saint-Maximin that miraculously arrived on the same day as the bowls I ordered from CB2 in the shape of a Vesica Pisces, and for being the kind of magical beings that make curious sympathies like this happen all the time

Laura McKowen & Elena Brower for our sacred text-trinity of poetry, and for the love we shared the day Mary Oliver died

Cynthia Bourgeault, Karen L. King, Jean-Yves Leloup, Hal Taussig, McGuckin & Hyung Chung for your academic prowess, your spiritual brilliance, and continued inspiration

Jeffrey Pettis, Jeffrey Mansfield & Jeffrey Kripal for helping me see that I've always been in love with a Christianity that hasn't been tried yet

"Penny" for teaching me the prayer of the heart, and for showing me how excited I can choose to be in any moment about what's next (even or especially since I don't know what's next)

Kyle Gray for putting up with all my skinny-dipping in the White Spring (both times,) and for loving me so fiercely and completely I can actually feel it all the way from Glasgow to Cleveland

Kate "The Good Witch" Northrup for the Just Love sweatshirt you got me, for crying, dancing, and laughing with me at Omega, for reminding me that ladylove is what will save the world, or at least, our love never fails to save mine

Glennon Doyle & Abby Wambach for following the voice of truth inside you, and for finding each other

Tres from Sacred Hour for helping me with the pain in my left side from my neck to my knee so I could keep writing, and for being not just a massage therapist but a healer

Dr. EJ Zebro for tying a red thread together for the last several months of writing this book, and for being such a beautiful man

Tammy Valicenti for our EMDR work together that made so much more possible for me

ABOUT THE AUTHOR

MEGGAN WATTERSON is the author of *REVEAL, The Sutras of Unspeakable Joy,* and *The Divine Feminine Oracle* and the co-author of *How to Love Yourself (and Sometimes Other People).* She is a feminist theologian with a Master of Theological Studies from Harvard Divinity School and a Master of Divinity from Union Theological Seminary at Columbia University. Meggan facilitates the REDLADIES—a community of radical love that lets her preach about female saints, mystics, gurus, and poets who inspire and teach us to live in service of love. She leads retreats and workshops on the divine feminine, Mary Magdalene, and the soul-voice meditation. Her work has appeared in media outlets such as *The New York Times, Forbes, The Huffington Post,* and *Marie Claire.* She lives with her old-soul son and his exuberant goldfish, Bob.

Website: **www.megganwatterson.com**

Hay House Titles of Related Interest

YOU CAN HEAL YOUR LIFE, the movie, starring Louise Hay & Friends
(available as an online streaming video)
www.hayhouse.com/louise-movie

THE SHIFT, the movie,
starring Dr. Wayne W. Dyer
(available as an online streaming video)
www.hayhouse.com/the-shift-movie

***

DISRUPT-HER: A Manifesto for the Modern Woman, by Miki Agrawal

EMPOWERING WOMEN: A Guide to Loving Yourself, Breaking Rules, and Bringing Good into Your Life , by Louise Hay

OWN YOUR GLOW: A Soulful Guide to Luminous Living and Crowning the Queen Within, by Latham Thomas

PUSSY: A Reclamation, by Regena Thomashauer

WITCH: Unleashed. Untamed. Unapologetic, by Lisa Lister

All of the above are available at your local bookstore,
or may be ordered by contacting Hay House (see next page).

***

We hope you enjoyed this Hay House book. If you'd like to receive our online catalog featuring additional information on Hay House books and products, or if you'd like to find out more about the Hay Foundation, please contact:

Hay House, Inc., P.O. Box 5100, Carlsbad, CA 92018-5100
(760) 431-7695 or (800) 654-5126
(760) 431-6948 (fax) or (800) 650-5115 (fax)
www.hayhouse.com® • www.hayfoundation.org

Published in Australia by: Hay House Australia Pty. Ltd.,
18/36 Ralph St., Alexandria NSW 2015
Phone: 612-9669-4299 • *Fax:* 612-9669-4144
www.hayhouse.com.au

Published in the United Kingdom by: Hay House UK, Ltd.,
The Sixth Floor, Watson House, 54 Baker Street, London W1U 7BU
Phone: +44 (0)20 3927 7290 • *Fax:* +44 (0)20 3927 7291
www.hayhouse.co.uk

Published in India by: Hay House Publishers India,
Muskaan Complex, Plot No. 3, B-2, Vasant Kunj, New Delhi 110 070
Phone: 91-11-4176-1620 • *Fax:* 91-11-4176-1630
www.hayhouse.co.in